ELIZABETH BOWEN

Modern Critical Views

Henry Adams
Edward Albee
A. R. Ammons
Matthew Arnold
John Ashbery
W. H. Auden
Jane Austen
James Baldwin
Charles Baudelaire
Samuel Beckett
Saul Bellow
The Bible
Elizabeth Bishop
William Blake
Jorge Luis Borges
Elizabeth Bowen
Bertolt Brecht
The Brontës
Robert Browning
Anthony Burgess
George Gordon, Lord
 Byron
Thomas Carlyle
Lewis Carroll
Willa Cather
Cervantes
Geoffrey Chaucer
Kate Chopin
Samuel Taylor Coleridge
Joseph Conrad
Contemporary Poets
Hart Crane
Stephen Crane
Dante
Charles Dickens
Emily Dickinson
John Donne & the Seven-
 teenth-Century Meta-
 physical Poets
Elizabethan Dramatists
Theodore Dreiser
John Dryden
George Eliot
T. S. Eliot
Ralph Ellison
Ralph Waldo Emerson
William Faulkner
Henry Fielding
F. Scott Fitzgerald
Gustave Flaubert
E. M. Forster
Sigmund Freud
Robert Frost

Robert Graves
Graham Greene
Thomas Hardy
Nathaniel Hawthorne
William Hazlitt
Seamus Heaney
Ernest Hemingway
Geoffrey Hill
Friedrich Hölderlin
Homer
Gerard Manley Hopkins
William Dean Howells
Zora Neale Hurston
Henry James
Samuel Johnson and
 James Boswell
Ben Jonson
James Joyce
Franz Kafka
John Keats
Rudyard Kipling
D. H. Lawrence
John Le Carré
Ursula K. Le Guin
Doris Lessing
Sinclair Lewis
Robert Lowell
Norman Mailer
Bernard Malamud
Thomas Mann
Christopher Marlowe
Carson McCullers
Herman Melville
James Merrill
Arthur Miller
John Milton
Eugenio Montale
Marianne Moore
Iris Murdoch
Vladimir Nabokov
Joyce Carol Oates
Sean O'Casey
Flannery O'Connor
Eugene O'Neill
George Orwell
Cynthia Ozick
Walter Pater
Walker Percy
Harold Pinter
Plato
Edgar Allan Poe
Poets of Sensibility & the
 Sublime

Alexander Pope
Katherine Ann Porter
Ezra Pound
Pre-Raphaelite Poets
Marcel Proust
Thomas Pynchon
Arthur Rimbaud
Theodore Roethke
Philip Roth
John Ruskin
J. D. Salinger
Gershom Scholem
William Shakespeare
 (3 vols.)
 Histories & Poems
 Comedies
 Tragedies
George Bernard Shaw
Mary Wollstonecraft
 Shelley
Percy Bysshe Shelley
Edmund Spenser
Gertrude Stein
John Steinbeck
Laurence Sterne
Wallace Stevens
Tom Stoppard
Jonathan Swift
Alfred, Lord Tennyson
William Makepeace
 Thackeray
Henry David Thoreau
Leo Tolstoi
Anthony Trollope
Mark Twain
John Updike
Gore Vidal
Virgil
Robert Penn Warren
Evelyn Waugh
Eudora Welty
Nathanael West
Edith Wharton
Walt Whitman
Oscar Wilde
Tennessee Williams
William Carlos Williams
Thomas Wolfe
Virginia Woolf
William Wordsworth
Richard Wright
William Butler Yeats

These and other titles in preparation

Modern Critical Views

ELIZABETH BOWEN

Edited and with an introduction by
Harold Bloom
Sterling Professor of the Humanities
Yale University

CHELSEA HOUSE PUBLISHERS ◇ 1987
New York ◇ New Haven ◇ Philadelphia

© 1987 by Chelsea House Publishers,
a division of Chelsea House Educational Communications, Inc.,
  95 Madison Avenue, New York, NY 10016
  345 Whitney Avenue, New Haven, CT 06511
  5014 West Chester Pike, Edgemont, PA 19028

Introduction © 1987 by Harold Bloom

Printed and bound in the United States of America

∞ The paper used in this publication meets the minimum
requirements of the American National Standard for Permanence
of Paper for Printed Library Materials, Z39.48-1984.

Library of Congress Cataloging-in-Publication Data
Elizabeth Bowen.
    (Modern critical views)
    Bibliography: p.
    Includes index. 46296
    Summary: Critical essays on the writings of
Elizabeth Bowen.
    1. Bowen, Elizabeth, 1899–1973—Criticism and
interpretation. [1. Bowen, Elizabeth, 1899–1973—
Criticism and interpretation. 2. English literature—
History and criticism] I. Bloom, Harold. II. Series.
PR6003.06757Z62 1987   823'.912   86-29873
ISBN 0-87754-641-X

Contents

Editor's Note

This book gathers together the best criticism that is available upon the writings of Elizabeth Bowen, reprinted here in the chronological order of its original publication. I am grateful to Vicki Forman and Susan Laity for their erudition and judgment as researchers.

My introduction centers upon three short stories which I take as representing Bowen at her strongest: "Sunday Afternoon," "Ivy Gripped the Steps," and "Mysterious Kôr." The chronological sequence of criticism begins with early readings of *The Death of the Heart* by the poet Mona Van Duyn and of *To the North* by William Heath which complement one another by finding, in different ways, that Bowen surprisingly achieves the illusion of realism through manipulating tightly controlled and elaborate artifice.

Edward Mitchell discusses the principal themes that bind together Bowen's stories, while Richard Gill enhances our sense of Bowen's social context, partly as set forth in her admirable *Bowen's Court*. A reading of *The House in Paris* by Harriet Blodgett praises the novel for its subtle control of form and myth, praise that might have been welcome to Bowen, who valued this rather too Jamesian performance over her other books. In a study of *The Heat of the Day*, Barbara Bellow Watson finds in this war novel a vision closer to that of Kafka and Beckett than to Jane Austen.

Hermione Lee, studying *A World of Love* and the two late novels, *The Little Girls* and *Eva Trout*, brilliantly elucidates Bowen's "bend back," her search for consolation in a return to her earlier years, a quest for lost time to counteract the alienation she felt in postwar Britain and Europe. Equally brilliant is the analysis of the relation between women and language in Bowen by Harriet S. Chessman, who finds in Bowen a subtle guilt of authorship that reflects the divide between women who possess language and women who do not.

Clare Hanson considers form in Bowen's short stories, a consideration that works to confirm Bowen's own emphasis upon vision, rather than feeling, in her best and most characteristic work. The book ends with the American poet Alfred Corn, reviewing a biography of Bowen, who arrives at the insistence that the Anglo-Irish novelist was one of the masters of modern fiction.

Introduction

Elizabeth Bowen, who died in 1973, seems not so widely read and discussed now as she was in earlier years when her major books were first published: *To the North* (1932), *The Death of the Heart* (1938), *Ivy Gripped the Steps* (1946), *The Heat of the Day* (1949). I have just completed rereading these three novels and *Ivy Gripped the Steps,* her best volume of short stories (called *The Demon Lover* in Great Britain). The novels retain their force and distinction, though the shadow of Henry James darkens their originality. More remarkable even than the novels are the stories, so much so that I am inclined to believe that, after James Joyce and D. H. Lawrence, Bowen may be the most distinguished British writer of short stories in our time. Three stories in particular have affected me so strongly upon rereading that I will confine this introduction to studying them: "Sunday Afternoon," "Ivy Gripped the Steps," and "Mysterious Kôr." Like Bowen's novels, the stories are in the mode of Henry James, in which what never quite happens is more nuanced and vital than anything that does take place. But the shadow of the Master flickers uncertainly in these three strong stories, all of which carry a force that is altogether Bowen's own.

Angus Wilson, in his shrewd introduction to Bowen's *Collected Stories,* locates this force in Bowen's elegant formalism, in her extraordinary aesthetic sensibility. That is certainly part of the matter; the economy and control of Henry James and James Joyce find a legitimate continuance in Bowen's art. Yet her stories seem to me to touch the sources of their power in ways more analogous to those of Lawrence in his stories. Like Lawrence, she has a considerable intimacy with the drives that Freud named Eros and Thanatos, and, again like Lawrence and Freud, she shows profound awareness of the labyrinthine ways in which these two antithetical drives contaminate one another in all of us. Bowen's superb control of craft and vision sometimes masks the extent to which she is a legitimate seer. Her force is so

1

overwhelming because her psychological insights are almost invariably accurate and persuasive, sometimes indeed uncanny.

II

"Sunday Afternoon," a story of less than seven pages, opens with the arrival at an Irish country house of forty-three-year-old Henry Russel, on holiday from his ministry in London during the Blitz, and from his bombed-out flat. He is visiting Mrs. Vesey and her friends, all a generation older than himself, in whose shadow he has grown up, and who have taught him their aesthetic of living, now uneasily vanishing from him even as he feels a nostalgia for its charm and for the fading appeal of its teachers.

A third generation enters the story with Maria, Mrs. Vesey's niece, an ardent young woman, impatient for life, for the war, for heroes, and so for London. Henry departs, after an immensely low-key yet highly revelatory exchange with his friends, who mourn the loss of all his "beautiful things," or, as he describes the victims of his destroyed flat, "some pieces of glass and jade and a dozen pictures." To Mrs. Vesey and her friends, the loss of these emblems of the aesthetic of living is the loss of life. Henry, in perfect understanding of the strength of their vision, nevertheless remarks that he would not have preferred to go into eternity accompanying the lost valuables: "But, in fact, I am very glad to remain. To exist." This subtle parting from his forerunners is the prelude to Henry's experience of the abyss between Maria, the next generation, and himself, which ends the story:

> "You know," he said, "when you come away from here, no one will care any more that you are Maria. You will no longer be Maria, as a matter of fact. Those looks, those things that are said to you—they make you, you silly little girl. You are you only inside their spell. You may think action is better—but who will care for you when you only act? You will have an identity number, but no identity. Your whole existence has been in contradistinction. You may think you want an ordinary fate—but there is no ordinary fate. And that extraordinariness in the fate of each of us is only recognized by your aunt. I admit that her view of life is too much for me—that is why I was so stiff and touchy today. But where shall we be when nobody has a view of life?"
>
> "You don't expect me to understand you, do you?"
>
> "Even your being a savage, even being scornful—yes, even that you have got from them.—Is that my bus?"

"At the other side of the river: it has still got to cross the bridge.—Henry—" she put her face up. He touched it with kisses thoughtful and cold. "Goodbye," he said, "Miranda."

"—Maria—"

"Miranda. This is the end of *you*. Perhaps it is just as well."

"I'll be seeing you—"

"You'll come round my door in London—with your little new number chained to your wrist."

"The trouble with you is, you're half old."

Maria ran out through the gates to stop the bus, and Henry got on to it and was quickly carried away.

Maria is Shakespeare's Miranda, abandoning Prospero's enchanted island. Henry, only a little in love with her, touching her upturned face with kisses thoughtful and cold, nevertheless takes care to kiss her more than once. Maria, only a little in love with him, half dismisses him with "you're half old," but half old is after all half young. Doubtless they will meet in London, and perhaps something will happen, but not much, since, for Henry, Maria's charm will abandon her quickly with the dying of her aunt's aesthetic of living, and Henry's charm, such as it may be for Maria, is only transitional, being an intimation of that dying into life which constitutes Maria's desire and which will surround her on every side in London.

What then has Bowen given us except nuance, bittersweet and intelligent? More, much more. All that matters in the story is her own surrogate, Henry, loyal to indomitable, blitzed London, and loyal also to Mrs. Vesey and her circle, to a view of life that can make every fate an extraordinary one, as Henry's is and will be, and as he fears Maria's will not be. The aesthetic of living here, Jamesian and Joycean, goes back to a common ancestor of both novelists and of their counterparts in Bowen and Virginia Woolf: the sublime Walter Pater. Sitting on Mrs. Vesey's lawn on a Sunday afternoon in late May, Henry has known another Paterian epiphany or privileged moment, a transfiguration by the accident of a sudden light:

Drawing a cane chair into the circle, he looked from face to face with concern. His look travelled on to the screen of lilac, whose dark purple, pink-silver, and white plumes sprayed out in the brilliance of the afternoon. The late May Sunday blazed, but was not warm: something less than a wind, a breath of coldness, fretted the edge of things. Where the lilac barrier ended, across the sun-polished meadows, the Dublin mountains continued to trace their hazy, today almost colourless line. The coldness had been admitted by none of the seven or eight people who, in degrees of elderly beauty, sat here full in the sun, at this sheltered edge of the lawn: they continued to master the coldness, or to deny it, as though with each it were some secret *malaise*. An air of fastidious, stylized melancholy, an air of being secluded behind glass, characterized for Henry these old friends in whose shadow he had grown up. To their pleasure at having him back among them was added, he felt, a taboo or warning—he was to tell a little, but not much. He could feel with a shock, as he sat down, how insensibly he had deserted, these last years, the aesthetic of living that he had got from them. As things were, he felt over him their suspended charm. The democratic smell of the Dublin bus, on which he had made the outward journey to join them, had evaporated from his person by the time he was half-way up Mrs Vesey's chestnut avenue. Her house, with its fan-lights and tall windows, was a villa in the Italian sense, just near enough to the city to make the country's sweetness particularly acute.

Fastidious and stylized, being secluded behind glass, as in a Paterian vision of crystal, Mrs. Vesey's circle yields to time's revenges, loses Maria to a life of mass identities, but goes on revolving in crystal. The expense of vision here is borne by the Jamesian hero-victim, Henry, who will never cease to be suspended between Mrs. Vesey and Maria, and will find no consort in his own transitional generation.

III

In just twelve pages, "Mysterious Kôr" is almost a novella, complete in its radical incompleteness as an action, as a complex sexual encounter that does not take place. We are in crowded, wartime London at the height of the Blitz, on the most extraordinary moonlit of moonlit nights. Arthur, on his first night of leave, wanders the chilly city with Pepita, but they have no place to go except the tiny flatlet she shares with Callie, who has not offered to vanish for the night: "Arthur was to have the sitting-room divan, usually occupied by Pepita, while she herself had half of her girl friend's bed."

That is exactly what happens. Nothing happens, yet everything takes place that can occur, psychologically and metaphysically. Even as the moon's siege of light unsettles besieged London, we apprehend everything that ever could be possible between Arthur and Pepita, Arthur and Callie, and, most subtly, Pepita and Callie. Arthur is a rueful realist, aware of his limitations and of Pepita's unappeasable otherness, her quest for a lover more imaginative than any lover, let alone Arthur, could hope to be. Here he speaks to Callie, after Pepita falls asleep:

> "It is really I who am putting you out," said Callie.
>
> "Well, that can't be helped either, can it? You had the right to stay in your own place. If there'd been more time, we might have gone to the country, though I still don't see where we'd have gone there. It's one harder when you're not married, unless you've got the money. Smoke?"
>
> "No, thank you. Well, if you're all right, I'll go back to bed."
>
> "I'm glad she's asleep—funny the way she sleeps, isn't it? You can't help wondering where she is. You haven't got a boy, have you, just at present?"
>
> "No. I've never had one."
>
> "I'm not sure in one way that you're not better off. I can see there's not so much in it for a girl these days. It makes me feel cruel the way I unsettle her: I don't know how much it's me myself or how much it's something the matter that I can't help. How are any of us to know how things could have been? They forget war's not just only war; it's years out of people's lives that they've never had before and won't have again. Do you think she's fanciful?"
>
> "Who, Pepita?"
>
> "It's enough to make her—tonight was the pay-off. We couldn't get near any movie or any place for sitting; you had to fight into the bars, and she hates the staring in bars, and with all that milling about, every street we went, they kept on knocking her even off my arm. So then we took the tube to that park down there, but the place was as bad as daylight, let alone it was cold. We hadn't the nerve—well, that's nothing to do with you."
>
> "I don't mind."
>
> "Or else you don't understand. So we began to play—we were off in Kôr."
>
> "Core of what?"
>
> "Mysterious Kôr—ghost city."
>
> "Where?"

"You may ask. But I could have sworn she saw it, and from the way she saw it, I saw it, too. A game's a game, but what's a hallucination? You begin by laughing, then it gets in you and you can't laugh it off. I tell you, I woke up just now not knowing where I'd been; and I had to get up and feel round this table before I even knew where I was. It wasn't till then that I thought of a cigarette. Now I see why she sleeps like that, if that's where she goes."

"But she is just as often restless; I often hear her."

"Then she doesn't always make it. Perhaps it takes me, in some way—Well, I can't see any harm: when two people have got no place, why not want Kôr, as a start? There are no restrictions on wanting, at any rate."

"But, oh, Arthur, can't wanting want what's human?"

Arthur's reply—"To be human's to be at a dead loss"—is the kernel of the young man, as Callie's "can't wanting want what's human?" gives us the essence of a generous if still untried young woman. Pepita indeed is dreaming of mysterious Kôr, where larger than human desires always can be fulfilled, and where the marvelous final paragraph of Bowen's story takes us:

Pepita had now turned over and lay with her face up. The hand that had struck Callie must have lain over the other, which grasped the pyjama collar. Her eyes, in the dark, might have been either shut or open, but nothing made her frown more or less steadily: it became certain, after another moment, that Pepita's act of justice had been unconscious. She still lay, as she had lain, in an avid dream, of which Arthur had been the source, of which Arthur was not the end. With him she looked this way, that way, down the wide, void, pure streets, between statues, pillars and shadows, through archways and colonnades. With him she went up the stairs down which nothing but moon came; with him trod the ermine dust of the endless halls, stood on terraces, mounted the extreme tower, looked down on the statued squares, the wide, void, pure streets. He was the password, but not the answer: it was to Kôr's finality that she turned.

Poor Arthur may always be the password for Pepita, but he will never be the answer. Her unconscious act of justice in striking Callie comes near the mark; Callie indeed is moved by Arthur, but Arthur, at a dead loss, is fit neither for mysterious Kôr nor for London in the Blitz, a loss which helps cause Callie's "loss of her own mysterious expectation, of her love for love." Subtlest is the stated, never realized relation between Pepita and Callie. Arthur, brooding on their unalikeness, catches them shrewdly: "Pepita so small, except for her too-big head, compact of childish brusqueness and of unchildish passion, and Callie, so sedate, waxy and tall—an unlit candle." The repressed element between the two, emergent in Callie's anticipatory and mediated desire for Arthur, is rendered by many details in the story. But no desire—repressed, mediated, overt—can be fulfilled in this story. As in "Sunday Afternoon," Bowen studies the siege of light upon her characters' erotic consciousness. What matters most between them cannot be acted out, cannot be said by them to one another or to themselves, cannot indeed be represented fully by Bowen. Her reticence reflects a previous era, now almost wholly lost to us. Its values would be lost also, if the best of her stories did not survive to help instruct us in what has departed. "Mysterious Kôr," a superb story by any standards, is now also a vision of what the return of the repressed has cost us.

IV

Angus Wilson has judged Bowen's "Ivy Gripped the Steps" to be "arguably her finest story," a judgment with which I agree; it is her masterpiece. In twenty-five pages, Bowen gives us not a story but a shapely novella, worthy of Henry James at his strongest, or of that other Jamesian disciple, the Willa Cather who wrote *A Lost Lady*.

The time is September 1944, when the affluent seaside resort town Southstone has just been declared out of the front line of the war zone. Gavin Doddington, a bachelor of forty-two, returns to Southstone merely to gaze upon a closed and sealed-up house, overgrown with ivy. The story's first sentence signals the pastness of the house's past: "Ivy gripped and sucked at the flight of steps, down which with such a deceptive wildness it seemed to be flowing like a cascade." Mrs. Nicholson, the rich, beautiful widow who had been the closest friend of Gavin's mother, had died in 1912, but her death had prolonged rather than ended the hopeless love that had developed in Gavin between the ages of eight and ten, when he had spent much time as Mrs. Nicholson's house guest, in order to improve his frail health in the better air of Southstone.

A Paterian epiphany or privileged moment marks the first confirmation that the boy Gavin has fallen hopelessly and irrevocably in love with Mrs. Nicholson:

The rule was that they, Rockham and Gavin, walked zigzag down by the cliff path, but travelled up in the lift. But one day fate made Rockham forget her purse. They had therefore to undertake the ascent. The path's artful gradients, hand-railed, were broken by flights of steps and by niched seats, upon every one of which Rockham plumped herself down to regain breath. The heat of midday, the glare from the flowered cliff beat up Gavin into a sort of fever. As though a dropped plummet had struck him between the eyes he looked up, to see Mrs Nicholson's face above him against the blue. The face, its colour rendered transparent by the transparent silk of a parasol, was inclined forward: he had the experience of seeing straight up into eyes that did not see him. Her look was pitched into space: she was not only not seeing him, she was seeing nothing. She was listening, but not attending, while someone talked.

Gavin, gripping the handrail, bracing his spine against it, leaned out backwards over the handrail into the void, in the hopes of intercepting her line of view. But in vain. He tore off clumps of sea pinks and cast the too-light flowers outwards into the air, but her pupils never once flickered down. Despair, the idea that his doom must be never, never to reach her, not only now but ever, gripped him and gripped his limbs as he took the rest of the path—the two more bends and few more steps to the top. He clawed his way up the rail, which shook in its socket.

The transparent face of Mrs. Nicholson, the unreal object of the boy's transcendent desire, provides the boy's "experience of seeing straight up into eyes that did not see him." They never do see him, as eventually he comes to know, a knowing that will inflict an immortal wound upon him, a kind of advanced narcissistic scar. If the story merely traced the subtle process of the boy's painful enlightenment, it would have been sufficient, but Bowen characteristically gives us a great deal more than that. Mrs. Nicholson has no particular aesthetic of living; she is little more than an amiable and mindless hedonist. Yet she has grace, charm, personal beauty, and an authentic period flavor; she too is a vision of a faded, lost world. Gavin is no Henry Russel, who is a man of considerable culture. Yet, like the hero of Bowen's "Sunday Afternoon," Gavin is in the void between two worlds, Mrs. Nicholson's and the A.T.S. girl he vainly approaches at the close of "Ivy Gripped the Steps."

I would locate the finest moment of "Ivy Gripped the Steps" in Gavin's disillusionment:

Gavin played for time, on the way down, by looking into the rooms on every floor. Their still only partial familiarity, their fullness with objects that, in the half light coming in from the landing, he could only half perceive and did not yet dare touch, made him feel he was still only at the first chapter of the mystery of the house. He wondered how long it would be before he saw them again. Fear of Rockham's impatience, of her calling down to ask what he was up to, made him tread cautiously on the thickly carpeted stairs; he gained the hall without having made a sound. Here he smelled the fresh-baked cakes, waiting in a hamper on the hall table. The drawing-room door stood ajar, on, for a minute, dead silence. The Admiral must have gone, without the cakes.

But then the Admiral spoke. "You must see, there is nothing more to be said. I am only sorry I came. I did not expect you to be alone."

"For once, that is not my fault," replied Mrs Nicholson, unsteadily. "I do not even know where the child is." In a voice that hardly seemed to be hers she cried out softly: "Then this is to go on always? What more do you ask? What else am I to be or do?"

"There's nothing more you can do. And all you must be is, happy."

"How easy," Mrs Nicholson said.

"You have always said that that was easy, for you. For my own part, I never considered happiness. There you misunderstood me, quite from the first."

"Not quite. Was I wrong in thinking you were a man?"

"I'm a man, yes. But I'm not that sort."

"That is too subtle for me," said Mrs Nicholson.

"On the contrary, it is too simple for you. You ignore the greater part of my life. You cannot be blamed, perhaps; you have only known me since I was cursed with too much time on my hands. Your—your looks, charm and gaiety, my dear Lilian, I'd have been a fool not to salute at their full worth. Beyond that, I'm not such a fool as I may have seemed. Fool?—all things considered, I could not have been simply that without being something a good deal viler."

"I have been nice to Constance," said Mrs Nicholson.

"Vile in my own eyes."

"I know, that is all you think of."

"I see, now, where you are in your element. You know as well as I do what your element is; which is why there's nothing more to be said. Flirtation's always been off my beat—so far off my beat, as a matter of fact, that I didn't know what it was when I first saw it. There, no doubt, I was wrong. If you can't live without it, you cannot, and that is that. If you have to be dangled after, you no doubt will be. But don't, my dear girl, go for that to the wrong shop. It would have been enough, where I am concerned, to watch you making a ninnie of that unfortunate boy."

"Who, poor little funny Gavin?" said Mrs Nicholson. "Must I have nothing?—I have no little dog. You would not like it, even, if I had a real little dog. And you expect me to think that you do not care . . ."

The two voices, which intensity more than caution kept pitched low, ceased. Gavin pushed open the drawing-room door.

The attentive reader has known for some time that the Admiral was Mrs. Nicholson's not wholly subservient lover. That reader could not have known how shallow, empty, pragmatically harmful Mrs. Nicholson was, taking poor Gavin as a substitute for "a real little dog." And the severe culpability of Mrs. Nicholson, lest we mitigate it, is driven home by Bowen at the very end of the story:

"I've got nobody to talk to," Gavin said, suddenly standing still in the dark. A leaf flittered past. She was woman enough to halt, to listen, because this had not been said to her. If her "Oh yes, we girls have heard that before" was automatic, it was, still more, wavering. He cast away the end of one cigarette and started lighting another: the flame of the lighter, cupped inside his hands, jumped for a moment over his features. Her first thought was: yes, he's quite old—that went along with his desperate jauntiness. Civilian, yes: too young for the last war, too old for this. A gentleman—they were the clever ones. But he had, she perceived, forgotten about her thoughts—what she saw, in that moment before he snapped down the lighter, stayed on the darkness, puzzling her somewhere outside the compass of her own youth. She had seen the face of somebody dead who was still there—"old" because of the presence, under an icy screen, of a whole stopped mechanism for feeling. Those features had been framed, long ago, for hope. The dints above the nostrils, the lines extending the eyes, the lips' grimacing grip on the cigarette—all completed the picture of someone wolfish. A preyer. But who had said, preyers are preyed upon?

His lower lip came out, thrusting the cigarette up at a debonair angle towards his eyes. "Not a soul," he added—this time with calculation, and to her.

"Anyway," she said sharply, "I've got a date. Anyway, what made you pick on this dead place? Why not pick on some place where you know someone?"

Gavin is a lifetime ruin, a mechanical amorist, a wolfish preyer, because of having been preyed upon by Mrs. Nicholson. He is indeed "a whole stopped mechanism for feeling," Mrs. Nicholson's victim. Yet he is also his own victim, for his visit to Southstone is more than an involuntary repetition of a trauma. From having been in love with Mrs. Nicholson, Gavin evidently fell in love with his own humiliation. The A.T.S. girl speaks his ironic epitaph: "Anyway, what made you pick on this dead place? Why not pick on some place where you know someone?" The wolfish preyer will come back to this dead place, will return to where he knows no one. Gavin commemorates Mrs. Nicholson's mindless yet memorable and criminal deed by inflicting upon himself a boredom comparable to hers. Perhaps Bowen's ultimate point is that Mrs. Nicholson was not so very culpable after all. At least Gavin sincerely loved her, and so encountered the single, if one-sided actual emotional event of his life.

At the close of *Bowen's Court,* her eloquent chronicle of her ancestral home and of her family throughout the Irish centuries, Bowen wrote, "There is a sort of perpetuity about livingness, and it is part of the character of Bowen's Court to be, in sometimes its silent way, very much alive." "Ivy Gripped the Steps" is a story about just the opposite, showing us that there is a sort of perpetuity about deathliness, and warning us aesthetically and morally against such a fate.

MONA VAN DUYN

Pattern and Pilgrimage: A Reading
of The Death of the Heart

Because *The Death of the Heart* has been read almost exclusively as a realistic narrative of adolescent initiation, there is probably no pressing obligation to spend critical time on that aspect of its success. But calling attention to another of its aspects does seem necessary in order that the peculiar nature of Elizabeth Bowen's achievement be understood. I know of no other novel with so tight and studied a patterning of characters, setting, narrative organization and prose style which has yet so successfully maintained the illusion of realism. Readers who are concerned with the resources of fiction must, I think, recognize and give credit to the skill which allows it to operate here with such duplicity. Miss Bowen has exercised a rigor of selection from the details of common-sense reality which we have come to expect from one major mode in fiction, yet has maintained a narrative surface which remarkably minimizes the distortions of it to which Joyce, Faulkner, Woolf and their heirs have accustomed us. It is to the rigor of selection, the formal ordering, that I would like to direct belated critical attention in this reading.

Six of the seven main characters are linked to each other in a geometric pattern whose clarity is concealed by the author's talent for individuation and our consequent faith in each as a human entity. "Innocent" is the label the novel supplies for a quality of mind and feeling in one trio, Portia, Eddie and Major Brutt. Each represents a different kind of innocence: Portia, 16, the natural innocence of youth; Eddie, 25, that of severe emotional wound-

From *Critique: Studies in Modern Fiction* 4, no. 2 (Spring/Summer 1961). © 1961 by *Critique*.

ing, effemininacy; Major Brutt, 45, that of blindness, failure of imagination. The second trio, Anna, Thomas and St. Quentin, are joined by their common quality, experience or commitment. Of the possible kinds of commitment, three are represented: marriage—Anna; business—Thomas; art—St. Quentin. Further, each member of the first group is paired with one in the second in order that, by means of comparison, the individual kind and degree of allegiance to the common quality may be illuminated: Portia with Anna; Eddie with St. Quentin; Thomas with Major Brutt. Five of the characters are fixed in their emotional stance, so the story, the movement which engages our hopes and fears, has to do with Portia's progress toward the natural loss of innocence involved in growing up. The impact of this movement on the three "experienced" characters delineates a flaw in the adjustment each has made to maturity, the extent to which the "loving nature" which Portia represents in extreme and "in vacuo" has been thwarted or defiled in them by experience. The impact of Portia's passage on the members of her own group is likewise recorded; it shakes, in the case of Eddie, and destroys, in the case of Major Brutt, the makeshifts by means of which the older innocents have managed to get by in the world. The problem the novel poses by its interrelationships of characters is whether Portia in particular, or since there is no representative of success, anyone, can manage this perilous journey without the death of the heart. Other aspects of the writing—style, organization, and descriptive detail—enlarge and enrich this theme.

Portia, Thomas Quayne's half-sister, is on the one hand a figure like the existentialist heroes in Sartre who can take no perception for granted, and on the other hand an ordinary adolescent whose problem of learning how grown-up society operates is aggravated by the peculiar character of her heritage and upbringing. Her ignorance of ordinary behavior is so great that her whole being is concentrated on a search for clues in the relationships between people she knows. "Either that girl or I are mad," Anna Quayne tells St. Quentin after reading Portia's diary, and the purity of her quest, her "hundred failures to take the ordinary cue" do combine to constitute a kind of madness. "Each of us keeps, battened down inside himself, a sort of lunatic giant—impossible socially, but full-scale—and . . . it's the knockings and batterings we sometimes hear in each other that keeps our intercourse from utter banality. Portia hears these the whole time; in fact she hears nothing else," St. Quentin says. She cannot seem to learn "why people said what they did not mean, and did not say what they meant." She comes to feel, in the aftermath of explosions she precipitates, that "there is no ordinary life." Through Portia's sympathetic identification with "the little suffering Anna" of the childhood drawing at the Heccombs', we see that Anna may once have been as vulnerable, as open to experience as Portia herself, and we can measure the distance that she has moved from such vulnerability. With Anna "feeling was by now unwilling," but she has "resonance." She knows that experience is not meaningful until it begins to repeat itself; she knows, that is, what she by now is. Experience has imposed on her the answer to the question posed for Portia: in the heart there is no ordinary life. Can one learn the ropes of social intercourse, with its necessary discrepancies and dishonesties, can one assume a manner of operation which gives other persons the security of knowing what to expect, and can one accept the same blanknesses, half-lies and weaknesses in others and still maintain the extraordinary life of the heart? For Anna the answer is no. Hurt by the failures of her career, her love affair with Pidgeon and her attempt to have children, she closes herself off from further vulnerability. She keeps her husband Thomas at an emotional distance and amuses herself with a safe flirtation with Eddie, and a safe friendship with St. Quentin. These two will never endanger her by coming close. Such desperate husbanding of feeling may be one of the many possible results of the journey to adulthood which Portia is beginning.

The second innocent, Eddie, has a "young debauched face" which can look "strikingly innocent" because no experience has really touched him, and which conceals "the vacuum inside of him." He acts, not out of feeling, but out of what he thinks people expect of him, continually going wrong and disrupting relationships because he has no real connection with people and so misjudges their wishes. He is malicious, catty, a wicked mimic; he also has "no sense of proportion, thank God"; his handwriting is, to the "simple eye" of Mrs. Heccomb, disarmingly unmasculine. Living on others, flirting with them, hating them, trying to protect himself from their touch, he has no notion of what he is except as he sees himself reflected in other eyes. Portia's last look at him gives him an unbearable picture—"I may be some kind of monster." The facts that Eddie has written a novel and that he and St. Quentin are Anna's two chosen friends link him with the novelist; they define each other by their similarities and distances. There are emotional likenesses. Anna detects "a touch of malice in [St. Quentin's] pity for women." He "detest[s] intimacy, which [has] brought him nothing but pain," and he doesn't wish to know "what people think." Human beings have no spontaneous wish for each other, he feels, but manage to get along together by following the rules of social tact. Eddie's novel was an instance of a literary form's being used as vengeance upon the world, and was made possible by cleverness rather than knowledge. It's savage glitter came from his "freedom to say things about life that [others are] too deeply involved to say." For St. Quentin, writing is a way of life, and a total and successful one; he has found his manner of commitment in a profession that offers traditional sanctuary for the half-open heart. Style, he believes, may save one— that is, may mediate between unbearable reality and a bearable distortion of it. He has intellectual qualities which Eddie's hysteria will never permit him to have, insight into others, knowledge, even a limited kind of wisdom. He has the fullest self-awareness of any of the characters, as well as an articulateness which allows him to express self-definition.

The third of the innocents, the "idealistic old warthog," Major Brutt, is kind, honest, blundering, disconnected from life by both temperament and circumstance. Because the very extravagance and imperceptiveness of his ideals unfit him for genuine relationships, he is "a born third." He sees only the surface; he *never* hears the knockings and batterings, which are truly there. The sentimental chromo pictures into which people group themselves in his mind grotesquely differ from reality. He is unable to catch the emotional or intellectual drift of a gathering, being himself guileless to the point of half-wittedness. When he and Thomas confront each other in the latter's study to discuss business, we see that each is what the other might easily have become. Thomas has a certain heaviness of mind, but he is saved from being the totally unimaginative man by his unrequited passion for his wife. He is open to no one else, however, but fortifies himself with blankness in his study and "has no idea what people feel." "We are minor in everything but our passions," he thinks. He is not the thinking man, but he too knows what he is. He has fitted into his father's firm, is solidly committed to it, but is repelled by the cynicism and suspiciousness that business has produced in him, and by the "competitiveness and funk" which seem to him all there is in it. Major Brutt, helplessly trying to enter some sort of business without a foothold, filled with childlike notions of there being something going on that "all you people are excited about," is shocked by and unable to believe the picture Thomas gives him of English middle-class business activity.

Portia's passage among the experienced causes them to suffer further emotional self-definition. Her gaze and presence remind Anna of her own defect in loving, and drive her still further from intimacy with Thomas and the girl: "She makes me feel like a tap that won't turn on." Portia's honesty, based on uncorrupted feeling, causes St. Quentin to see nostalgically how much he has lost by trading social honor—the agreement between people who care little for each other not to cause trouble for each other—for genuine honor, the total risk of caring. He breaks free of the former for a moment to enter Portia's heroic plane by betraying Anna and his own carefully maintained personality in the matter of the diary. The failure of his house to absorb Portia's presence points up to Thomas the weakness of his marriage, and leads him to see that "the way we live is hopeless." Authorial comment tells us that the "queasiness" of Windsor Terrace comes from its attempt to deny a vulnerability implicit in relationships with others, a denial which is doomed to failure in the lives of those who live in the world. Thomas finds relief from this uneasy "watchfulness" in love, and so "love[s] without any of that discretion known to more natural natures—which is why astute men are so often betrayed." And Portia brings destruction to the innocents. As long as she can remain a child Eddie can be with her, they can play games of affection, the terrible infant can show off to his adoring peer. But when she wants the whole of him, through love, he goes to pieces, for "the Eddie inside" can be given to no one. When Portia destroys Major Brutt's picture of life at the Quaynes, telling him he is the "other person they laugh at," the whole structure of his tenuous relationship to the world comes down. He sees "what a fiction was common-sense," "how specious wisdom was." His image of himself and others shatters, the illusions which give him "the nice way [he] see[s] things" collapse. He is left with nothing.

The seventh main character, Matchett, the housekeeper, is the only figure for whom realistic characterization is modified to surround her with an aura of symbolic importance. The whole force of Miss Bowen's descriptive talent goes to establish her as portentous, larger-than-life. She represents tradition, and is the character most purely "used" in controlling the theme. Matchett "came with the furniture" from Thomas's family to Windsor Terrace, and offers a continuous critique of the flimsy bulwarks it throws up against life. Matchett knows about people and houses; she is fooled by nothing. She sees how inadequate are the ways Thomas and Anna have chosen "to pass a thing off," such as birth and death. There are traditional patterns, ceremonials and habiliments for life's occasions, and Matchett despises those who have cast them off to stand on their puny, naked individualities. Her relationship to objects, her daily and seasonal observances of house care are ritualistic, religious: "She served the idea of sleep with a series of little ceremonials . . . the impassive solemnity of her preparation made a sort of altar of each bed; in big houses in which things are done properly, there is always the religious element."

Matchett stands for the non-churchly traditional observances by means of which human beings can come to feel a sense of relationship to nature, to the past and to other human beings, which allow "feeling to thicken" without destruction or disorientation. She is a fictional relative of Dilsey, in *The Sound and the Fury*, although the Quaynes, a modern self-sufficient family, feel the need of her services only once, for a symbolically important journey to fetch Portia home. Matchett's further wisdom is that no one is pure possibility, that each is more and more, as the years pass, the shaped product of what has gone before. St. Quentin tells Portia that "if one didn't let oneself swallow some few lies, I don't know how one would ever carry the past." Matchett, however, tells straight truths to Portia about her past, and, after Portia cries, feels that "something has been appeased." Matchett represents a means by which realities may be faced and innocence may move to maturity, a means which still functions, though it has been almost completely discarded. For the Quaynes it functions at a time when St. Quentin's knowledge is impotent.

The minor characters, because of the deftness and individuality with which they are drawn, satisfy one kind of novelistic expectation; they *exist* in all their multiplicity and appear because they are connected by background or proximity to the main characters. At the same time, however, they are as firmly held to the pattern of controlling idea as the major figures.

The sentimental, girlish widow, Irene, whose extra-marital affair with Thomas's father produced Portia, knew that "nine times out of ten the things you do direct from the heart are the wrong thing, and that she was not capable of doing anything better." Mr. Quayne was "all nature," an innocent old duffer. From this combination we get Portia's undiluted wish to love. Thomas's mother, Mrs. Quayne, "had no nature" and meant always, not to do good, but to do right. She was a "sacrificer," a self-congratulating pillar of righteousness—from the combination of Mr. and Mrs. Quayne we get the divided nature of Thomas. Lillian is a foil for Portia. (The humor of her characterization, by the way, is one of the delights of the book.) She represents the romanticist, the self-dramatizing, uninnocent connoisseur of her own emotions. Portia's genuine innocence is made luminously clear as she stands beside that voluptuary of sentiment. Mrs. Heccomb is the modern substitute for a Matchett, a simple-minded woman who served as ineffectual chaperone for Anna. Parallels between her bumbling attempts to guide Portia and Matchett's firm and confident ones are clearly drawn, particularly in the handling of Portia's letters from Eddie. The collection of characters at Waikiki (the Heccombs' cottage) is a little Shakespearean microcosm of society writ with humorous largeness and extravagance of statement because of its youthful unguardedness. The most Mrs. Heccomb can do in presiding over it is to preserve some faint intermittent semblance of propriety, to keep Waikiki, that symbol of modern life at its most naked and inept, from blowing right off the coast and into the sea under the nerve-wracking assaults of animal spirits, impermanence of structure and buffetings of nature. Daphne is the female representative of gross discrepancy between verbal decorum and vulgarity of feeling, and Dickie is the masculine equivalent. Clara is the victimized innocent. Mr. Burseley is the coarse "male" counterpart to Eddie (Portia tries to resist this identification) and Cecil is an adolescent St. Quentin.

Descriptions of places in *The Death of the Heart* surround the action of the novel with visual testimony to its authenticity and at the same time play a carefully selected role in developing the theme. The book examines the possibility of losing innocence, entering upon and engaging in adult life, while yet maintaining fullness of heart, and it is one of its premises, "stated" through these descriptions of places, that relationship to the past is a crucial problem to be solved before such a future can be envisaged. Objects and houses are symbols of that relationship, mirrors of individual solutions, adequate or inadequate. "Pictures would not be hung plumb over the centres of fireplaces or wallpapers pasted on with such precision that their seams make no break in the pattern if life were really not possible to adjudicate for. These things are what we mean by civilization . . . in this sense, the destruction of buildings and furniture is more palpably dreadful to the spirit than the destruction of human life."

Windsor Terrace, the house which reflects Thomas's and Anna's imperfect solution, which Matchett presides over and contemptuously holds up to a vanished ideal, which Mr. Quayne saw as the last stronghold of solid family life, and through which, not Thomas's child, but Portia moves like the Young Pretender, is pretty, airy, vivacious. It represents taste rather than tradition: "Family custom, partly kind, partly cruel, had long been rationalized away." Matchett's hand "seemed to support the fragile Regency pillar," though she is neither consciously needed nor wanted there. Anna cares how things look—she dares not care too much how they are. And appearances succeed with the naïve Mr. Quayne and Major Brutt, as well as, by unspoken social agreement to look away from depths and chasms, with St. Quentin. Anna is successful in editing life, nothing more: "no one seemed clear what was being discarded, or whether anything vital was being let slip away. If Matchett were feared, if she seemed to threaten the house, it was because she seemed most likely to put her thumb on the thing."

St. Quentin's rooms are not described; he has found his place in literature, an alternative, if not wholly life-fulfilling house.

The three "innocents" have, in a sense, no homes. Portia comes from a life in flats and hotels. She has no relationship to Things, to furniture and a house, to help her know "what [she] was meant to be." Eddie's furnished room has "the unadult taste of college rooms" filled with "stark objects one does not possess." To the smell of carpet and ashes and dust and stagnant tea, the rotting stems of flowers left over from the last time he entertained a woman add their symbolic stink. To this place Portia, in her premature flight from childhood at Windsor Terrace, comes first to seek an adult home. And Major Brutt's room at the Karachi Hotel, to which she is drawn next by her unerring sense of those who are "the same" as she, is no better equipped to receive her. The Karachi is a down-at-the-heels "warren," filled with those who, like Major Brutt, are hanging onto the economic and emotional edge of life. Everything creaks. The unchosen closeness of human beings to each other makes "love or talk indiscreet." At the very top, in the attic where he lives at a cut price, there is more privacy because the rooms are too small to be further divided up. Portia's physical presence jams the room. There is nowhere for her to sit.

Waikiki, setting for the speeded-up entrance of Portia into social relationships and the crisis of her attachment to Eddie, is a sounding box for the thrashing about of animal energy. Built not for the rearing of families but for the vacations of strangers, it is lived in by the Heccombs only part of the year. When Portia first catches sight of it, one window has blown open, a faded curtain is wildly blowing out and the bell is hanging out of its socket. People bang on the door and yell for entrance. It has an almost transparent front. Furniture has the vulgar gloss of varnish, like Daphne's veneer of verbal gentility (and unlike the waxed pieces Matchett cares for, whose rubbed sheen comes from generations of loving or unloving effort). The electric light "pour[s] down with a frankness unknown to Windsor Terrace." Sounds and smells continuously remind its inhabitants of one another's physicality. Dickie crashes about like a giant loose in the house, bath water runs out noisily, waste gurgles in the pipes, the roasting joint smells, Doris, the maid, smells. And the house lets in as well the damp of sea air and the smell of brine. Yet, as it creaks and strains and shifts under the coast wind, it stands with an almost shiplike strength, as if it might manage to float even if cut loose from the land and set adrift on the chaos of nature. With those whom it suits, the sturdy and coarse-natured, the novel is not primarily concerned, though these, it suggests, may be the only undamaged survivors of a wholly "modern" life.

It would be too cumbersome to give a full reading of that close patterning which extends to the book's descriptive details, its organization and its style. Maturity, the necessary compromise between the heart and the world, the spirit and the flesh, innocence and knowledge, may be achieved with the help of various mediators, among them tradition (social patterning) and art (personal patterning), Miss Bowen suggests throughout. The first paragraph, for example, touches lightly but firmly, through objective-seeming description, on motifs which reappear through the book. It is winter, and the scene is brittle and burnished. We are in a formal park, with a pond in which swans swim in channels of dark water between segments of ice. But, significantly, "a sort of breath from the clay, from the city outside the park, condensing, made the air unclear." Seasons of the year order the stages in Portia's emotional growth. The cycle of human life is linked to the cycle of seasons in the case of Portia, the developing person; emotional states are linked to the seasons in the cases of those characters who are already developed. We first meet Portia at the premonition of spring in London (the breaking ice), we see her go through a precocious springtime in the seashore weather (the Quaynes, as well as Portia, are away from Windsor Terrace while Matchett conducts alone her ritualistic spring cleaning, whereby the care of life's furnishings is brought into rhythm with nature) and there is a significant intimation of summer at the end of the novel. The park serves as symbol of the formal ordering which one way of life imposes on nature (in contrast to the straggling formlessness of walks and the combustion of relationships which nature imposes on the human way of life at Waikiki) and consequently as a setting in which Thomas, Anna and St. Quentin stroll and talk in dignified circles (Portia walks blindly, is nearly run over). A "breath from the clay, from the city outside" suggests a commercial civilization which threatens the "park" way of life, but also, and more basically for Portia's story, represents the facts of existence—sexuality, mortality—with which a civilized ordering must come to terms, which it must take into full account lest it squeeze life out of the heart.

One's relationship to objects and houses is sign and symbol of the kind of pact one has made with reality, the novel posits. Therefore the feelings of the experienced characters color our sight of physical premises. (Portia's untutored eye and heart are incapable of meaningful response to what she sees, and so authorial intercession does most of the work of showing the reader what attitude he must take while Portia views the scene—Eddie's room, Major Brutt's room, Windsor Terrace; only at Waikiki, openness and helplessness, does Portia's response fully appear, since her experience has prepared her to see this most accurately.) When Anna walks with St. Quentin in the park, expressing her unwillingness to go back inside to live in the critical self-awareness induced by Portia's presence, the houses appear as follows: "At the far side of the road, dusk set the Regency buildings back at a false distance: against the sky they were colourless silhouettes, insipidly ornate, brittle and cold. The blackness of windows not yet lit or curtained made the houses look hollow inside." But St. Quentin, who comes to his friends to feed egotistically on surface comforts and agreeableness, untouched by deeper troubles, continues on his walk with reluctance: "he threw a homesick glance up at Anna's drawingroom window. Inside, he saw firelight making cheerful play. . . . Ahead lay the knolls, the empty cold clay silence of inner Regent's Park beneath a darkening sky." St. Quentin is intellectually more perceptive to the "cold clay" silence of the park and to the "darkening" of its sky than the other characters are. Later in the book, when Thomas brings Anna and those two innocent viewers, Portia and Major Brutt, back from the movies, Thomas feels a sudden premonition of the emptiness which lies behind the appearances of his home: he "felt round for his key. As though he heard himself challenged, or heard an echo, he looked sharply over his shoulder down the terrace—empty, stagey, E-shaped, with frigid pillars cut out on black shadow: a façade with no back. 'We're wonderfully quiet up here,' he told Major Brutt," and the Major's kindly and imperceptive gaze accepts that self-assurance as total truth.

The titles of the novel's three sections enlarge the operation of the theme by setting it in a traditional framework. The three temptations which the medieval mind saw as a threat to saintliness, perfect innocence and purity of heart—the World, the Flesh and the Devil—the modern mind sees as aspects of experience which must be mastered in order to produce a fullness of humanity: not the saint, but the warm yet competent social person. So Portia, our hope for undamaged capacity to love and live in the secular life, meets them one by one. Her encounter with the World, represented by Windsor Terrace, is characterized by a company of imperfect guides and representatives who surround her there. In place of parents she has Thomas and Anna—the first incapable of bearing the pressure of any need upon him but his wife's, the second embarrassed and inadequate, unable to offer affection, steering a haphazard course which misses giving her either the security of being treated as a child or social guidance in being treated as a young lady. For girl friend she has Lillian, perverse emotionalism; for boy friend, Eddie, superficial and malicious distortion of interpretation. From the avuncular Major Brutt she gets toys, while Matchett, handicapped by lack of authority, conspires against Anna to give her her inheritance of memory—her own past—and the support of "custom." The Flesh, Waikiki, presents her with Mr. Burseley's hand on Daphne's bottom, his leering "Anyone ever told you you're a sweet little kid," Eddie's fingers kneading Daphne's hand because he feels "matey," the drunken fiasco at the Pavilion, and Mrs. Heccomb's comically incompetent efforts at chaperonage. The Devil, whose instrument is St. Quentin, brings her down in the ancient manner, with knowledge. She has been by no means readied to face the truth, its "fantastic universe," its "unseemliness and glory." "I suppose it's better to know," she says to St. Quentin, who replies, "No, truly it is not. In fact I've done something to you I could not bear to have done to myself. And the terrible thing is, I am feeling the better for it." As she falls, she in turn brings down Eddie, pathetically unequipped to deal with emotional truth, and Major Brutt, even more pathetically unprepared to deal with intellectual truth.

Both characterization and idea are enriched by a series of parallels and contrasts which lie under a life-like descriptive surface. For example, there is the contrast between St. Quentin's attitude toward the past and Matchett's, in their differing efforts to tell Portia how to meet the world: St. Quentin, "Memory is quite unbearable enough, but even so it leaves out quite a lot." Matchett: "They'd rather . . . not have the past. No wonder they don't rightly know what they're doing. Those without memory don't know what is what." Or, the symbolic difference between Portia's diary and St. Quentin's books. As Anna says, "[It] was not a bit like your beautiful books. In fact it was not like *writing* at all." Portia's diary is to literary art as Portia herself is to the maturely functioning person she may or may not become. It is a pure register of happening, the unmitigated, unbearable, inquiring stare at experience. Its childish sentence structure represents its method—all clauses, that is, all observations, entered without discrimination or judgment of importance or relationship. This is a way of seeing which cannot survive, and it is a way of mirroring which other people cannot stand (Eddie, who "breaks every rule every time," gets a malicious pleasure out of reading it, but insists that nothing be written about him; Portia is "God's spy," St. Quentin tells her). The truth of literature is quite different from the truth of innocence. "You've got to allow for style . . . there are ways and ways of trumping a thing up: one gets more discriminating, not necessarily more honest. I should know, after all," St. Quentin says. A discriminating style of recording—art—shapes and illuminates one's knowledge of reality; a discriminating style of living, the goal of Portia's pilgrimage, shapes and illuminates one's experience of it.

Miss Bowen's own style, though it is characteristic of all her novels, functions with particular appropriateness in this story as a further support of the theme. Action and description are interrupted, so frequently as to enforce the technique upon the reader's attention, with passages of essay, "set pieces" of generalization in which truisms of human experience are sensitively recorded. As the characters undergo their individualized moments of insight or ordeal, the novel holds these up against a background of knowledge drawn from observation of how "we," the human family, tend to respond in such situations. A moment of action, for example the one in

which Major Brutt is losing one of the rosy pictures of other lives by which
he lives and is beginning to build up a new and even rosier picture of the
happy little family at Windsor Terrace, is accompanied by the following:

> A man must live. Not for nothing do we invest so much of
> ourselves in other people's lives—or even in momentary pictures
> of people we do not know. It cuts both ways: the happy group
> inside the lighted window, the figure in long grass in the orchard
> seen from the train stay and support us in our dark hours. Illu-
> sions are art, for the feeling person, and it is by art that we live, if
> we do. It is the emotion to which we remain faithful, after all: we
> are taught to recover it some other place.

Lillian's sympathizing with Portia's catastrophe is accompanied by a long
essay, which begins:

> There is no doubt that sorrow brings one down in the world.
> The aristocratic privilege of silence belongs, you soon find out,
> to only the happy state. . . . With its accession to full power,
> feeling becomes subversive and violent: the proud part of the
> nature is battered down. Then, those people who flock to the
> scenes of accidents, who love most of all to dwell on deaths or
> childbirths or on the sickbed from which restraint has gone smell
> what is in the air and are on the spot at once, pressing close with
> a sort of charnel good will. You may first learn you are doomed
> by seeing those vultures in the sky.

It is as if, by the narrative method itself, the novel asserts a necessity for
setting individual happening in a larger context of social experience. Against
that it gains dignity and meaning, against that it leans as a child leans on its
family, and from that its personal character most fully emerges. Portia, who
feels "anything that happens has never happened before. What I mean is,
you and I are the first people who have ever been us," is right. But so is
Major Brutt when he says, "We all take these knocks." Common-sense,
wisdom (which Major Brutt, under the onslaught of Portia's candor, sees, in
a terrible vision, as mere makeshifts and fictions) carry one only part way
(the essay can never substitute for the novel). But they modify the loneliness
of the human heart and make its uniqueness bearable.

We are not shown in the novel's action whether Portia can "come
back" to achieve the womanliness, intelligence and charm of her Shakespearean namesake, for whom traditional wisdom, to which she was bound
in choosing a husband, so happily corroborated the heart's spontaneous

wish. ("But why was she called Portia?," St. Quentin asks. "Anna, surprised, said 'I don't think we ever asked.' ") Such a wound may turn her into an Anna who is tempted to toss Pidgeon's letters at Portia and tell her, "This is all it comes to, you little fool." First she must come back to Windsor Terrace, dependence, and later make a perhaps more fortunate re-beginning of her adult life. It is clear to the reader that the Quaynes have done the right thing by sending Matchett to fetch her, and that Matchett is the only remaining means of helping her.

Matchett, treated through most of the novel as a looming and awe-inspiring figure, is given, in the final scene of the taxi ride to the Karachi, the full weight of humorous and fallible humanity. This "downfall" sets limits on her power, though she opens the hotel door "with an air of authority." Tradition, custom, the personal and communal past, the novel suggests, are supports only, not mystical or magical maps for the course of the grown-up life.

Does loss of innocence lead to the death of this particular, but representative, heart? The title is unequivocal. "Happy that few of us are aware of the world until we are already in league with it," says the author, and Portia's awareness was catastrophically premature. Yet the reader who has learned to find a weight of meaning in descriptive detail is left with this final suggestion:

> In the Karachi Hotel drawing-room, someone played the piano uncertainly.
>
> All the same, in the stretched mauve dusk of the street there was an intimation of summer coming—summer, intensifying everything with its heat and glare. In gardens outside London roses would burn on, with all else gone in the dusk. Fatigue but a sort of joy would open in all hearts, for summer is the height and fullness of living. Already the dust smelled strong. In this premature night of clouds the sky was warm, the buildings seemed to expand. The fingers on the piano halted, struck true notes, found their way to a chord.

WILLIAM HEATH

The Jacobean Melodrama
of To the North

Almost as a deliberate act of conscious rejection, Miss Bowen abandoned what she has called the "muted Elizabethan world" of Jane Austen in favor of the violent actions in the melodramatic Jacobean terror of *To the North*. When the restraints in tone and the limitations on relevant action are removed, the effect is a boundless world in which the reader must ever more desperately seek his own position. In effect, *Friends and Relations* involved the working out of a relatively abstract problem, the paradox arising when the family tree simultaneously embodies the orderly salvation of the tree of Jesse and the destructive chaos of the tree of good and evil. By this rather calculated means, the family love of relations conflicts with the romantic affinity of friends, and the conscious ironic tone of the novel is even reflected in the title, for few here are "friends," and "relations" are more often the potential concerns of divorce suits than the participants in family reunions.

To the North, however, had an appropriately less rational genesis. Miss Bowen has said that she first conceived the "idea" of the novel when, driving outside London with her husband, she suddenly saw a road sign reading "To the North" outlined against the sky. And the novel that takes its form from this image is equally (and deliberately) nonrational in statement: in the midst of a realistic, modern London an innocent girl, Emmeline, is seduced by a Satanic villain, Markie, and brings about his death and hers when no alternative action is possible, the fire of their passion somehow creating the ice of their destruction. The author states this inevi-

From *Elizabeth Bowen: An Introduction to Her Novels.* © 1961 by the Regents of the University of Wisconsin. University of Wisconsin Press, 1961.

27

tability, from the point of view of Markie, in language as extravagant as the events it describes:

> She [Emmeline] had, as he saw, stepped in Paris clear of the every-day, of conduct with its guarantees and necessities, into the region of the immoderate, where we are more than ourselves. Here are no guarantees. Tragedy is the precedent: Tragedy confounding life with its masterful disproportion. Here figures cast unknown shadows; passion knows no crime, only its own movement; steel and the cord go with the kiss. Innocence walks with violence; violence is innocent, cold as fate; between the mistress's kiss and the blade's is a hair's-breadth only, and no disparity; every door leads to death. . . . The curtain comes down, the book closes—but who is to say that this is not so?

In this novel, however, the action does not take place in the relative isolation of an Italian hotel, an Anglo-Irish Big House, or an English Abbey, for Emmeline, an orphan, lives in a carefully described house in St. John's Wood with her widowed sister-in-law, Cecilia Summers, and manages a travel bureau in Bloomsbury. Her immersion in the midst of the everyday is contradicted by her attitude toward her environment. Her nearsightedness is repeatedly emphasized, and this physical defect is symptomatic of a similar psychological one, for "she was short-sighted in every sense. Watching slip past her a blurred, repetitive pattern she took to be life, she adored fact—the exact departure of trains—and had taught herself to respect feeling." Emmeline's dedication to the travel bureau, then, is her attempt to join vicariously in the experience of others, compensating for the psychological retreat she herself has made and for the passivity of her acquaintances. In spite of her adoration of fact and action, her spiritual home is the country estate, appropriately named Farraways, of her cousin Lady Waters where "grief was a language she did not know" and she can feel that "free will was a mistake but did not know what this meant."

> Here Emmeline, stepchild of her uneasy century, thought she would like to live. Here—as though waking in a house over an estuary to a presence, a dazzling reflection: the tide full in—she had woken happy. But already a vague expectation of Monday and Tuesday filled her; looking out from the shade of the lime already she saw the house with its white window-frames like some image of childhood, unaccountably dear but remote.

Though Emmeline as the "stepchild of her uneasy century" can see life steadily and whole only in a retreat from London to childhood, Markie is

decidedly the natural son of a dislocated age who is most at home in the flat
he occupies in his sister's house in Lower Sloane Street where he and his
sister "made a point of not meeting, cut each other's friends at the door, had
separate telephone numbers and asked no questions" and where his only
communication with the rest of the house is the speaking tube through
which he whistles to the cook for meals. Visiting a country house for him is
an experience not of peace but of hell:

> No birds sang: it had been worse than that day in Keats. Leaves,
> rotting and rusty, deadened his steps; the afternoon had been
> sodden and quite toneless; it began to be dark early. Down there,
> between the dreary trunks of the beeches, houses lay like a sedi-
> ment in the cup of the misty valley: great gabled carcases, villas
> aping the manor, belfried garages where you could feel the cars
> get cold.

The alliance between Emmeline and Markie is without volition, almost
fated. Markie has the *beauté du diable* Miss Bowen has mentioned in Henry
Crawford of *Mansfield Park,* and the predilection for the innocent virgins
attracted by this quality. Cecilia, meeting him on a train headed north to
England from Italy, is able to perceive immediately in his "mobile, greedy,
intelligent mouth and the impassive bright quick-lidded eyes of an agreeable
reptile" a potential nemesis: "in an afterworld, she might deserve just such a
companion: too close, glancing at her—if any shreds of the form still clung
to the spirit—without sympathy, with just such a cold material knowingness." The diabolism that the serpent imagery here suggests is further supported by Markie's other characteristics: he is incapable of satisfaction in
any relationship, opposes churches as "oppressive monument[s] to futility," and enjoys the pursuit and corruption of Emmeline far more than her
passive physical surrender to him, for then he misses

> that precious sense of delinquency lovers enjoy. It was in the idea
> of outrage, of those tender agonies of the conscience, that he was
> most a voluptuary: the idea of guilt so enflamed him that the
> form surrendered in innocence seemed as cold as marble.

If Markie is the devil of the novel, Emmeline is obviously its angel, a
title she is given with almost annoying frequency. It is Markie's pet name for
her, the basis of frequent metaphors used to describe her, and when she feels
there is no way out of her relationship with Markie she becomes an angel of
death. This encounter between devil and angel, linking the good and the
evil, echoes the basic pattern of Elizabethan (or, better, Jacobean) tragedies,
a note initially struck by the opening description of Markie quoted above. In

addition to her sense of Markie's diabolism, Cecilia finds his description of
Rome to evoke "the late Renaissance, with a touch of the slick mondanity of
Vogue."

> Though not, evidently, a son of the Church, he was on the
> warmest of terms with it; prelates and colleges flashed through
> his talk, he spoke with affection of two or three cardinals; she
> was left with a clear impression that he had lunched at the
> Vatican. As he talked, antiquity became brittle, Imperial col-
> umns and arches like so much canvas. . . . The sky above Rome,
> like the arch of an ornate altarpiece, became dark and flapping
> with draperies and august conversational figures.

Once the reader is aware of an Elizabethan pattern within the novel, it is
easy enough to see in this language, with its metaphors of the theater, the
aura of intrigue surrounding the evil churchmen of Webster and Shirley.

The melodramatic pattern is most insistently apparent, however, in the
sequence of actions that accomplish Emmeline's downfall. Confrontation,
seduction, fall, realization, failure of outside help, failure of outside revenge,
and the inevitable self-sacrificing murder are its abstract stages; and a discussion of a few of them in detail can indicate what the Elizabethan and
theological levels add to a realistic modern novel.

The formal beginning of the seduction takes place, symbolically enough,
in the garden of Emmeline's house where the early morning invasion by the
cat from next door, "a noted *flaneur* in other gardens" and "one rippling
curve of malignity" prefigures the unexpected arrival of Markie, "pale and
puffy in a dishevelled white tie," still awake from the night before. His motive
for coming is itself feline (curiosity) and his presence among the light and
flowers, like that of the cat, is decidedly incongruous:

> Till now, she had offered to no friend her hours outside time:
> now the budding magnolia, plucked and discarded, breathed its
> unmeaning fragrance among the fumes of coffee. . . . For here
> Markie was: in his presence—within reach, if he cared to kiss, of
> his kiss, within reach, if she dared to put out a hand, of his
> hand—this idea of pleasure as isolated, arctic, regarding its own
> heart only, became desolating to Emmeline as a garden whose
> flowers were ice. Those north lights colouring the cold flowers
> became her enemies; her heart warming or weakening she felt at
> war with herself inside this cold zone of solitude.

This invasion of her private world and her unresisting acquiescence
(because she "desired lowness and fallibility") are the first steps toward the

downfall itself, which takes place in the hotel room in Paris, where Emmeline has gone to establish a business agreement with two Serbs who operate a continental travel agency. The arrangement, to be less formal than a partnership, they have called "interplay," and like the chess game in *Women Beware Women* or the card game in *A Woman Killed with Kindness,* the onstage discussion of interplay becomes a metaphor for the off-stage action in which Emmeline becomes Markie's mistress. Actions in this novel, indeed, are rarely to be seen as isolated events, for they can have analogues on almost any level. At the moment of Emmeline's surrender in Paris, Cecilia, at Farraways (unaware to the end of the novel of her sister-in-law's alliance), watches the sky:

> Somewhere, the moon was rising. Somewhere, clear of earth's shadow, the radiant full moon received the whole smile of the sun. Clouds hid from the earth at this bridal moment her lovely neighbour, while to the clouds alone was communicated ecstasy. . . . Clouds closed in; the moon did not appear; darkness spread over the skies again; only the lime and a wet path silver for less than a moment had known of the moon's rising. The tree and path faded; cloudbound while that tide of light swept the heavens earth less than suspected the moon's perfection and ardour. . . .
> "Perhaps," said Cecilia, "there is a moon in Paris."

Though her treatment of this moment may seem to justify O'Faolain's objection that "when Elizabeth Bowen is dealing with elemental things she skirts around them with too much elegance," it is clear that the fall of Emmeline is being echoed, almost elegiacally, on several levels at the same time—at a business luncheon, in a hotel room, and in the heavens above the earth. The richly suggestive imagery that would be present in the language of a Webster character is, in the freer extension of the novel, presented as metaphorical action.

The second stage in Emmeline's progress toward destruction, her realization that she has no escape, is similarly presented in several metaphorically related incidents, all concerned with the dissolution of her private world. During the weekend spent with Markie at a friend's cottage (which contains a large gold harp), Emmeline's realization that her affair with Markie has become dissociated from the rest of her life is presented by a description of landscape and setting:

> A little smoke from their fire dissolved in the clear evening; the downs in their circle lay colourless under the sky. Some childish idea of kind arms deserting her mind, Emmeline said: "How alone

we shall be tonight." Like a presence, this cold stillness touched
the idea of their love: would they dissolve like the smoke here,
having no bounds? The low roof was comforting, but the cottage
door, open, showed darkness where they had been.

When she hears that Cecilia is to be married and that the vicar of Farraways
is dead, and knows that the half of her life which had existed separate from
Markie is gone, again the metaphysical coordinates of tangible property are
used to suggest that disintegration is both physical and psychological:

Timber by timber, Oudenarde Road [the house in St. John's
Wood] fell to bits, as small houses are broken up daily to widen
the roar of London. She saw the door open on emptiness:
blanched walls as though after a fire. Houses shared with women
are built on sand. She thought: "My home, my home."

At the novel's least successful moments such attempts at symbolic extension become obviously linguistic, almost puns. "Falling to bits" too easily refers to houses, psyches, lives, and minds. At the same time that Markie,
bored with the complete control he has over Emmeline because she loves
him, reestablishes his liaison with his former mistress Daisy, Emmeline,
totally deserted, so exactly reenacts the disintegration the other girl had
gone through that Emmeline's secretary can tell her that

"You should take a rest. . . . You look all to bits." . . . Broken up
like a puzzle the glittering summer lay scattered over her [Em-
meline's] mind, cut into shapes of pain that had no other character.

The fluidity of this world, the fact that its essence is so conveniently
controlled by the metaphors the narrator uses to construct it, makes possible
the melodramatic climax. When Emmeline drives Markie toward Baldock
after the dinner party to which Cecilia and her fiancé Julian have invited him
under the assumption that he and Emmeline are still friends, Emmeline
becomes the Elizabethan bride of death. In an entirely unreal world, she
does not even bother to reject his offer to take her back, even marry her:

A sense of standstill, a hush pervaded this half-seen country.
Friendly darkness, as over a pillow, and silence in which a clock
striking still pinned her to time hung trancelike over this early
halt in their journey. But, from beyond, the North—ice and un-
breathed air, lights whose reflections since childhood had bright-
ened and chilled her sky, touching to life at all points a sense of
unshared beauty—reclaimed her for its clear solitude.

The scene is a corollary of the one in the garden where she deserted the "cold zone of solitude," and within the syntax of the sentences identity is lost in flux, so that darkness is "friendly," silence is "trancelike," and the abstract North performs a human action. An awareness of the inevitability of her destruction through Markie becomes clear to her, she is blinded by knowledge, and loses self. The only action, a slight one, results in destruction:

> Like earth shrinking and sinking, irrelevant, under the rising wings of a plane, love with its unseen plan, its constrictions and urgencies, dropped to a depth below Emmeline, who now looked down unmoved at the shadowy map of her pain. For this levitation a total loss of her faculties, of every sense of his presence, the car and herself driving were very little to pay. She was lost to her own identity, a confining husk. Calmly, exaltedly rising and balancing in this ignorance she looked at her hands on the wheel, the silver hem of her dress and asked herself who she was: turning his way, with one unmeasured swerve of the wheel, she tried to recall Markie.

At the moment she drives the small car head-on into the large one, she experiences for the first time a completely objective awareness, and the event itself is neither Emmeline's suicide nor her deliberate punishment of a transgressor, but the translation of the irrationality of her love into the physical actions of her life. Emmeline ceases to exist personally and socially, and becomes a force. It is this inevitable, nonhuman force, the release of energy from fire burning and ice forming, that destroys both of them.

But a summary of the plot, however it emphasizes the melodramatic nature of the novel, ignores much of its more rational content. Like an Elizabethan play, the novel has its subplot, in which the practical sister-in-law Cecilia accepts the passive Julian Tower as her second husband. The marriage is rather obviously related to the social compromises of the romantic will prevalent in the other novels. Cecilia, unable to love completely, nevertheless recognizes that she has an existence only in terms of other people. Julian, whom she accepts without love, is similarly unable to form any relationship based on feeling, and like Cecilia suffers from solitude. Although both Cecilia and Julian are able to rescue themselves, they can do nothing to save Emmeline. Julian, who knows that Markie has seduced her and that he should perhaps play the brother with the whip, can feel only envy of Markie "for cutting so much ice."

Thus Cecilia and Julian, the prosaic lovers, are ironic alternatives to the passionate lovers. Cecilia refuses to take Markie seriously, seeing his roles as *âme damné* and Byronic hero as mere poses, and in Julian's adolescent niece, Pauline, the subjective innocence of Emmeline herself is parodied. Having discussed the seventh commandment and "impure curiosity" at her confirmation class, Pauline "still could not think of anything without blushing. . . . So that now flowers made her blush, rabbits made her blush excessively; she could no longer eat an egg. Only minerals seemed to bear contemplation."

The other characters who inhabit the London circles that intersect those of Cecilia and Emmeline are apparently intended to represent more bizarre disorientations of feeling. Lady Waters keeps a salon of unhappy lovers, whose lives she further complicates under the guise of being helpful; Emmeline's business partner Peter is followed by a "haggard friend," apparently homosexual; and the stenographer resigns in bitter tears because Emmeline does not return her passionate devotion.

The unification of the melodramatic main plot, the ironic subplot, and the background comedy is brought about by the predominant metaphors of traveling. A large proportion of the action takes place on something that is moving, and by which, like fate, the characters are moved. Cecilia's meeting Markie on the train from Italy, and later driving with Julian to meet Pauline at her school, illustrates the correctness of Lady Waters's comment that "Cecilia . . . never seems to be happy when she is not in a train—unless, of course, she is motoring." The more significant traveling, however, is that done by Emmeline and Markie. The plane trip to Paris during which Emmeline verbally assents to Markie's demands is made symbolic of their moral position:

> She was embarked, they were embarked together, no stop was possible; she could now turn back only by some unforeseen and violent deflection—by which her exact idea of personal honour became imperilled—from their set course.

And to Emmeline, as a nearsighted angel, the sky is a native element, where theory can become principle and the restrictions of the world can be ignored, where "some new plan of life, forgotten between flight and flight, seemed once more to reveal itself." However, after her actual surrender in Paris, Emmeline is disturbed by movement because it threatens an idealized world where her romantic will can be realized, and she "now stood still with her hands on the bark of a tree in St. Cloud . . . bark whose actual roughness blurred to the touch at the thought of so many forests, and longed to stand still always."

But of course the most significant journey of all for Emmeline (who

likes Paris taxis because "they're like 'The Last Ride Together' ") is the one
that is literally the last ride together for her and Markie. The description of
this journey, moreover, clarifies much of the travel imagery in the rest of the
novel. Although Emmeline for the first time is ostensibly in control of what
is moving, she feels her actions entirely controlled by circumstance. After
she has seen the sign portentously pointing "To the North" and "something
[gives] way,"

> An immense idea of departure—expresses getting steam up and
> crashing from termini, liners clearing the docks, the shadows of
> planes rising, caravans winding out into the first dip of the des-
> ert—possessed her spirit, now launched like the long arrow [on
> the sign]. The traveller solitary with his uncertainties, with ap-
> prehensions he cannot communicate, seeing the strands of the
> known snap like paper ribbons, is sustained and more than him-
> self on a great impetus: the faint pain of parting sets free the
> heart.

The "great impetus," Fate, the North, is basically circumstance, constructed
of space and time. As she is driving, Markie stares at "the two lit dials: the
clock, the speedometer."

Though it is in and through time and space that a person constructs his
identity, to surrender to their abstract measures, minutes and miles, is finally
to destroy oneself. In her search for permanence (whether its outward form
be marriage, the house she shares with Cecilia, or the bark of a tree),
Emmeline seeks an identity in something immune to time, for only in this
way can she counteract the fantasy of subjectivity to which her "nearsightedness" restricts her. In her psychological concern with Emmeline,
Miss Bowen emphasizes her inability—partly because of her subjectivity,
partly because of the society around her—to find a permanent relationship
with the members of that society or to see her identity reflected in anything
that exists apart from time and motion. And as a student of society, Miss
Bowen seems to be demonstrating that this dislocation is common to all
(most of the characters are orphaned, widowed, unhappily married, or
incapable of feeling), so that only those who suppress the romantic will and
accept the outward forms of permanence as a duty that cannot be subjected
to the test of the romantic will can survive.

On a moral level, the issues raised in this novel are similar to those
considered in *Friends and Relations*. Emmeline, the angel of goodness, can
conquer the serpent only by sacrificing herself, by cutting down the tree of
knowledge which is also the tree of Jesse. The idealist, the romantic, the

subjectivist, perishes: Cecilia and Julian, in their prose without passion, with their existentialist realism, inherit the earth and the last remnants of Emmeline and Markie: the forgotten white scarf and rejected gloves.

For the first time in a novel Miss Bowen dramatizes the dilemma of the romantic will in a form that takes both society and morality into account. The reader is never told whether Sydney's road did indeed lead to an empty town, what replaced the burned shell of Danielstown, or who lived along the new road pegged out by the surveyors at the end of "The Disinherited." Yet Cecilia (one is tempted to see her, like Stella in *The Heat of the Day,* as a personification of Miss Bowen's attitude) is able to give the new life a habitation and a name. The passage, though long and undramatic within its context, is significant enough to be quoted in full:

> When a great house has been destroyed by fire—left with walls bleached and ghastly and windows gaping with the cold sky— the master has not, perhaps, the heart or the money to rebuild. Trees that were its companions are cut down and the estate sold up to the speculator. Villas spring up in red rows, each a home for someone, enticing brave little shops, radiant picture palaces: perhaps a park is left round the lake, where couples go boating. Lovers' lanes in asphalt replace the lonely green rides; the obelisk having no approaches is taken away. After dark—where once there was silence a tree's shadow drawn slowly across the grass by the moon, or no moon, an exhalation of darkness— rows of windows come out like lanterns in pink and orange; boxed in bright light hundreds of lives repeat their pattern; wireless picks up a tune from street to street. Shops stream light on the pavements, upon the commotion of late shopping: big buses swarm to the kerb, small cars dart home to the garage, bicycling children flit through the birdless dark. Bright façades of cinemas reflect on to ingoing faces the expectation of pleasure: lovers laugh, gates click, doors swing, lights go on upstairs, couples lie down in honest beds. Life here is liveable, kindly and sometimes gay; there is not a ghost of space or silence; the great house with its dominance and its radiation of avenues is forgotten. When spring is sweet in the air, snowdrops under the paling, when blue autumn blurs the trim streets' perspective or the low sun in winter dazzles the windows' gold—something touches the heart, someone, disturbed, pauses, hand on a villa gate. But not to ask: What was here?

The casual reader might see here a tone of unabashed nostalgia, even deliberate snobbery. After all, the symbols of aristocracy and gentle living—the
silence, darkness, trees, estates, obelisks, and "lonely green rides"—have
been obliterated by the raucous bourgeois evils: speculators, villas, picture
palaces, pink and orange lanterns, façades, garages, buses, asphalt, and
wireless. But to one who reads the passage this way, the verbs at least must be
vaguely puzzling, for the trappings of the new society emerge with an admirable vitality: brave and radiant, they spring up, stream, swarm, dart, flit. The
ambivalence of tone is resolved finally into an attitude more of welcome than
resignation, for the windows *are* gold and spring *is* sweet. Though the speaker
elevates herself when she refers to the "couples [who] lie down in honest
beds," there is little denigration implied and, we can assume, something does
"touch the heart." "Life here is liveable, kindly and sometimes gay": for
someone who *does* remember "what was here," these must be words of high
praise. Such a landscape, suggesting attitudes and details from almost all the
major stories and novels between 1929 and the war, is nevertheless an
incomplete statement. However successfully Cecilia manages to live by limit-
ing her vision, Miss Bowen's later heroines do repeatedly ask the destructive
question, and for people with their comprehensive knowledge more complex
forms of forgiveness must be found. Fortunately in the later novels the saving
illusion is not merely the negative absence of memory and perception but the
positive presence of knowledge and art. What Miss Bowen here accomplishes
with rhetoric, she later achieves with art.

EDWARD MITCHELL

Themes in Elizabeth Bowen's Short Stories

Treating the representative majority of an author's short fiction is not the most congenial of critical undertakings. Such an endeavor invites organization by exclusion, or inclusion at the expense of organization. The fact that here we are dealing with a modern British author who is extremely conscious of the history and development of the short story, as well as her own powers as an artist and a craftsman, makes the task no easier. Perhaps the most that can be hoped for from a discussion of this kind is an indication of the thematic patterns which link the collections of stories and a suggestion of the range of vision indicated by the variations within those patterns.

One situation to which Elizabeth Bowen consistently devotes her attention is the antithesis between external fact and internal reality, between the objective condition and the projection of an internal world where feeling alone reigns. Innocence in the world of Experience is in Miss Bowen's short fiction not so much the nexus around which the story is developed as it is the situation from which the story progresses. In the novel *The Death of the Heart* (1938), St. Quentin attempts to explain the position of the innocent: "I swear that each of us keeps, battened down inside himself, a sort of lunatic giant—impossible socially, but fullscale—and that it's the knockings and batterings we sometimes hear in each other that keeps our intercourse from utter banality. Portia hears that the whole time; in fact she hears nothing else." The "giant battened down" then is virtually ever present; what Miss Bowen explores is the state of the relation between the romantic

From *Critique: Studies in Modern Fiction* 8, no. 3 (Spring/Summer 1966). © 1966 by the Bolingbroke Society, Inc.

imagination—innocence, the giant—and the objective reality to which it ultimately must become reconciled.

In such a story as "All Saints" we are presented with a humorous instance in which the giant is definitely not battened down. Mrs. Barrows, "childlike" and "perennial," offers the astonished vicar an enormously expensive stained glass window because it "makes one feel so religious and good." Her unconventional and subjective view of saints and helpfulness reduces the vicar to stuttering out platitudes of orthodoxy: "Error . . . force of example . . . simply a manifestation." Unable to "place" Mrs. Barrows or her offer in any of the accepted conventional contexts, the vicar in desperation turns "on his heel and [flees] through the darkness."

The effects of an unwitting innocence like Mrs. Barrows's, preserved through life, are not always so innocuous either for the innocent or her victims. A slightly less happy instance is portrayed in "Mrs. Moysey." This secretive little woman who "looks like Christmas Eve every day" is hardly aware of, and little concerned with, the faults of her nephew, Leslie, who unexpectedly arrives to pay her an extended visit. When Leslie suddenly disappears and is replaced by Emerald, the wife he has deserted, with her two small children, Mrs. Moysey absorbs the children—"a bubble or two, some ripples that widened and vanished, then once more above them, its unruffled surface of tranquil secretiveness." Mrs. Moysey, as always, remains locked in her bedroom but the presence of the children there turns her life into "a long agitation, a flutter of happiness." The retreat, however, is not inviolate for Emerald returns, and forcing her way into the bedroom finds the children smeared with chocolate amid a mountain of empty candy boxes listening to Mrs. Moysey's life story, which, the little woman admits, she has touched up here and there. Emerald, "devoid of illusion, sharp with practical understanding," breaks into tears, and Mrs. Moysey, "most unwilling vicar . . . most unconvinced voluptuary," does "not know where to look."

Mrs. Moysey attempts to preserve her innocence behind a locked bedroom door. Amid a confused heap of empty chocolate boxes, she gives unbridled rein to her romantic imagination by writing a doctored account of her own life story. But the door will not remain locked and eventually Mrs. Moysey is made to face some of the less sugary facts of her own situation. Yet, although Mrs. Moysey and Emerald are "shattered" by their final confrontation, one is not led to believe that the damage Mrs. Moysey has done to her victims is irreparable. Preserved innocence can, however, lead to cruelly ruined lives as it does, for example, in "Queer Heart." Hilda, though middle-aged, is another innocent. Her face, although embedded in fat, is "as exposed and ingenuous as a little girl's," and she cannot "cure [herself] of the habit of loving life"; but she is an alien in her own home, the victim of what she feels is a "conspiracy" between her daughter Lucille and her sister Rosa.

After the death of Mr. Cadman, Rosa began "flapping round Granville like a doomful bird," and now, dying in an upstairs room, Rosa exerts more influence than ever over the lives of mother and daughter. Yet Rosa's hatred for Mrs. Cadman, and her efforts at alienating mother and daughter stem, as even Mrs. Cadman realizes, from a desire "to protect the interests of Lucille." That Rosa has "a queer heart, eating [itself] out, thanking God for the pain" is undeniable; but when she confronts her sister in the sick room, Hilda Cadman comes to see that innocence, even the justifiable innocence of childhood, can be brutal, and that the naïveté, the irresponsibility, the "good time, the real good time" of a middle-aged woman, is not only without justification but appallingly destructive. Because she was once denied a Christmas doll, Rosa has taken Lucille; but the loss of Lucille was only possible because of Mrs. Cadman's "real good time," and too late she thinks "I did that to her [Rosa]; then what have I done to Lucille?"

The giant *not* battened down, innocence preserved, is then one of the thematic patterns in Miss Bowen's collections of short fiction. But this pattern has its corollary: innocence forcibly maintained, the giant in chains. The synthesis between the infinite desire of the romantic imagination and the restrictive pressures of objective fact may never be formed because the innocent is incapable of making the necessary connections between various parts of his experience; or it may never be formed because the innocent is never permitted to encounter an undiluted reality—he is constantly forced to play a role which is not of his own choosing. The giant in chains, innocence forcibly maintained, invariably leads to mental aberrations and destruction either real or symbolic.

One of the effects of being forced to play a role is manifest in "The Dancing Mistress." Miss James, who greets her endless dancing classes "with stereotyped little weary amused exclamations" is only a pupil and teacher for Madame Majowski:

All day long she was just an appearance, a rhythm; in studio or ballroom she expanded into delicate shapes like a Japanese "mystery" flower dropped into water. Late at night, she stopped "*seeming*" too tired to "be"; too tired to eat or to speak; she would finish long journeys asleep with her head on the pianist's shoulder; her sister received her with Bovril and put her to bed.

> Her eyebrows tilted outward like wings; over her delicate cheek-
> bones looked out, slightly tilted, her dreamy and cold eyes in
> which personality never awakened.

That her personality is never awakened is felt only too acutely by Lulu, the hotel secretary. His amorous interest in Miss James is dampened because he can find no "self" in her; he asks her "who's there? What's there? *Are* you, at all? I want you." But Miss James's "self" is only capable of being stirred when she is sadistically punishing one of her pupils, like Margery Manner-ing. Only then does the "unrealized self in her [make] itself felt, disturbing her calm with a little shudder of pleasure. A delicate pink touched her cheekbones, she thought of Lulu, she was almost a woman." But a dancing mistress is the only kind of mistress Joyce James can be; neither she nor Lulu are permitted to have any real selves—"It did not do for Lulu, who showed ladies into their bedrooms, or Joyce who spent hours in clumsy men's arms, to be patently man and woman; their public must deprecate any attraction."

Perversion is the essence of this story; natural and artificial are reversed here as are masculine and feminine names. Miss Peele, the piano player, whose hair is "polished against her skull like a man's," is glad they are out of the fading misty daylight and into the artificial light of the Metropole ballroom—"I'm so glad we've got back to artificial—it seems so much more natural, I think." In response to Lulu's charge of lack of feeling in Joyce, Miss Peele remarks, "we'll forget each other anyhow—that's nature." Be-cause the artificial is natural, because the stereotyped role is the only role permitted her, Miss James's "unrealized self" has only the twisted outlet of sadistic punishment and the release of troubled sleep in which she dreams of telling Margery Mannering, "I'll kill you, I'll kill you."

The result of keeping the giant in chains, of forcibly preventing a con-tact between the self and the world of fact which it must assimilate and attempt to control, is vividly presented in terms of its effects upon children. Geraldine in "The Little Girl's Room" has been allocated the role of "prod-igy" by her grandmother. Mrs. Letherton-Channing lies "ambushed in gen-tleness [and] watched like a lynx for the first tentative emanations of young genius." Tutors are brought to Geraldine, art objects of all kinds are placed before her "till life, for her willful fancy, became an obstacle race." But Geraldine, who tears the living center, the reproductive parts, from the hearts of flowers and crushes the bud of the strawberry, leaving only the calyx, takes part in a nightly ritual unknown to her grandmother. Alone in her room Geraldine calls up "the enemies" who by day are the obsequious hirelings of Mrs. Letherton-Channing, but by night are the "red passions" who approach Geraldine with "knives gleaming," and for whom she waits with "delicious anticipation."

In her "little Italy from Wigmore Street," Geraldine feels "security, feeling for her in the dark, [close] the last of its tentacles on her limbs," while she vainly calls up the masochistic fantasies which are the perverted result of her ardent desire to destroy the suffocating prison in which she is entrapped. But enforced innocence occasionally has its revenge as it does in "The Easter Egg Party." The Evers sisters have only one object in view when they invite Hermione to their house for Easter: "to restore her childhood to her." But Eunice and Isabelle themselves lead insular "unperplexed lives"; they know that such things as broken marriages occur, but they refuse to believe such things happen to anyone they know as well as Hermione's mother. These "successful nuns" still receive "intimations of immortality" in a social atmosphere characterized by "inexpensive sociability, liberal politic, shapely antique family furniture, 'interests,' enlightened charity." The enforced innocence to which they would subject Hermione is, like their own, an innocence *manqué*, out of touch with any real world. The facts of life from which the sisters would so sedulously guard Hermione—the cat's weaning of her kittens, the natural reproduction of the birds—are stereotyped, superficial, and irrelevant to a girl in whose eyes "existed an alien world of experience." It is love and attention that Hermione needs—"it was their attention she wanted; she collected attention like twists of silver paper or small white pebbles." When she finds it denied she strikes back by stealing the Easter eggs and disrupting the party. Hermione revolts from enforced innocence and retaliates by telling Eunice "you keep on making me take an interest in things, and you never take the slightest interest in me"; and finally she escapes from the sisters leaving "a sort of scar, like a flattened grave, in their hearts."

In another section of *The Death of the Heart*, the narrator, momentarily stepping out of the novel, says, "illusions are art, for the feeling person, and it is by art that we live, if we do." Living, then, becomes the "art" of forming that integration between the self and the world which neither allows the giant complete freedom nor attempts to entomb him by complete repression. But there always exists the possibility of the "illusion of art," the mistaking of the illusion for the art of a balanced integration. This is not a question of innocence, since one half of the equation, experience, the world of fact, has been obliterated. In this case the subjective vision bears no relation to a world outside itself because it recognizes no world outside itself, it is centripetal and self-sufficient. This is the world of hallucination where the terms *innocence* and *experience* are without meaning, because without reference. Here the "illusion" of synthesis has been largely or completely substituted for the "art" of synthesis, and this substitution comprises a second prominent thematic pattern in Miss Bowen's short stories.

The substitution of an illusion for reality may be so gradual, its causes so minute, that it passes nearly undetected, as in the story "Foothold." Having recently moved into a new home, with her children away at school, Janet finds that there is "the house, the garden, friends, books, music, letters, the car, golf when one feels like it, going up to town rather a lot." Yet as she tells their house guest, Thomas, "my life—*this* life—seems to have stretched somehow." Janet's life has "stretched" so much that it now includes a ghost, Clara, with which Thomas, Janet, and her husband Gerard are slowly becoming preoccupied. But the ghost seems to be Janet's special property, a mental set become palpable in the form of a presence, an idea which intrigues Thomas who "had guessed her [Janet] capable of an intimacy, something disruptive, something to be driven up like a wedge, first blade-fine, between the controlled mind and the tempered, vivid emotions." To Thomas the idea of Clara is just an idea, a "joke," something to be defined; but to Gerard the matter is more serious—"She's seeing too much of this ghost . . . she wouldn't if things were all right with her." And neither of them realize how "disruptive" the "intimacy" has become until, retiring after a late evening, they are both brought to a halt outside Janet's bedroom door as they hear her saying to Clara, "I can't bear it. How could you bear it? The sickening loneliness."

Unwittingly, Thomas has put his finger on the source of the illusion which has gained a foothold in Janet when he says, "I've a theory that absolute comfort runs round the circle to the same point as asceticism." Janet's "absolute comfort" has become "sickening loneliness" and only a supernatural presence is now capable of supplying her with any "intimacy." Illusion and the disruption caused in the mind entranced by it can, however, go far beyond the point of a foothold. In such a story as "Dead Mabelle" we witness a mind undergoing a complete dislocation from reality. William Stickford, who "never went with a girl," is "intelligent, solitary, self-educated, self-suspicious." Not a frequenter of the cinema, he is finally induced to see the famous Mabelle Pacey, and while he sits with "angry, disordered feeling" watching the black and white world of abstraction, he feels "as though she were a rising flood and his mind bulrushes." After this first encounter with Mabelle, William avoids his friends and makes secretive excursions to the suburbs, even to London, to see one after another of Mabelle's movies because "there was this thing about Mabelle: the way she made love." But suddenly, horribly, Mabelle is killed. For several weeks William is left to face her "absolute dissolution"; yet, for William, Mabelle is not gone, she is "perpetual, untouchable . . . you couldn't break that stillness by the fire; it could shatter time. You might destroy the film, destroy the screen, destroy her body; this endured. She was beyond the compass of one's mind; one's being seemed a fragment and a shadow."

Stumbling from one of the theaters to which he compulsively returns to witness the reruns of Mabelle's films, William puts out a hand in the darkness—"You're here. *You* know *I* know you're here, you proud thing! Standing and looking. Do you see me? . . . You're more here than I." His vision of Mabelle is now more real than himself. Alone, in his sitting room, in the presence of Mabelle, William is alive, but tomorrow at the bank "that abstraction behind the business of living was due to begin again." Robbed of his "power of being" by the image of Mabelle who "burned brightly on," William slips his hand, in unconscious imitation, into his bureau drawer; but there is no "gesture of pistol to temple, the trail of smoke fugitive over an empty screen" because the drawer is empty of what it should contain: "the means to the only fit gesture that he could have offered her."

William Stickford is capable of "living" only under the obsessive influence of the compelling, dramatic, but artificial cinema actress. Perhaps it is only by illusions that we live, if we do, but it is madness to live *only* in illusion. When his brightly burning hallucination is juxtaposed to the "shabby business of living," William turns to the hallucination; but the shabby business of living is not the only force capable of calling up worlds-within-worlds of hallucination. The inability to face reality may also stem from the fact that that reality has become too horrible to face. Miss Bowen devotes one entire collection of stories to such a reality: the chaos and upheaval of war. In her postscript to *The Demon Lover* collection, Miss Bowen notes that when "what was happening was out of all proportion to . . . faculties for knowing, thinking and checking up," people were led down strange paths in search of "indestructible landmarks in a destructible world." Hallucination and illusion provided such landmarks.

"Mysterious Kôr" is one of Miss Bowen's finer renderings of the hallucinations precipitated by war. She defends the hallucinations depicted in this and the other stories in this collection by saying that they "are an unconscious, instinctive, saving resort on the part of the characters: life mechanized by the controls of war-time, and emotionally torn and impoverished by changes, had to complete itself *some* way." For Pepita mysterious Kôr is that "*some* way," because it represents the isolation, the withdrawal from time and reality, that are impossible for her and Arthur in an overcrowded and war-torn London. In a world which is "disenchanted," Kôr represents that place where "there is not a crack in it anywhere for a weed to grow in," and where "the stairs and arches are built to support themselves." Yet Kôr, like the moonlight which drenches London, obliterating niches and shadows as if they were "dissolved in the street by some white acid," is sterile, empty, dead.

Trapped in a world they are incapable of understanding, without a "place to be alone," frustrated in their attempt to enjoy a love which is largely "a collision in the dark," Pepita and Arthur unwillingly return from a walk through the deserted London streets to the small flat Pepita shares with her roommate, Callie. Callie, like her Hindu namesake, sacrifices the last of their frustrated passion on the altar of her "good manners" and "forbearance." Without a boy friend, stiff in her own virginity "like an unlit candle," she does not understand Pepita's attraction to the solitude of mysterious Kôr and she demands "Can't wanting want what's human?" But Arthur tells her that "to be human is to be at a dead loss." For Pepita and Arthur, both "at a dead loss," Kôr represents the only world which can still be grasped by the imagination. For Pepita, however, it goes beyond this. Kôr is both a product of the desiccated world and the final symbolization of Pepita's desire to escape into nonentity. Arthur is the source but not the end of her dream, "he was the password, but not the answer: it was to Kôr's finality that she turned."

Mental aberration, perfidious ignorance, abortive love are facts which the individual must recognize without being defeated by them. When the romantic imagination is unable to adjust its subjective vision to the world outside itself, dislocation, aberration, destruction are the consequences. But these same results may be produced not so much by the "batterings and knockings" of the giant subjective self as by the deterioration of accepted social patterns, the crumbling of moral values, a shift or upheaval in that objective world outside the self. This is not the failure to make a synthesis, but rather the failure of a synthesis to conform to the external "facts" which have themselves changed. This is the plight of the disinherited, who can place between themselves and a fallen world neither the shield of their own innocence nor the closed door of hallucination. Their plight forms another of the basic thematic patterns in these short story collections.

One of the processes of familial and moral disinheritance is revealed in "The Man of the Family." William, whom his Aunt Luella playfully calls "the man of the family," stops at her Regent's Park house on his way from Oxford to London because his aunt "kept an excellent table." He basks in the warmth of his aunt's admiration and feels "solid" in a family where there are never any grievances. But William suddenly finds his solidity and comfort disrupted by his involvement in his cousin Patsey's third engagement. William's difficulties begin when another cousin, Rachel, tells him that the fiancé, Chummy, "is not a nice man." Rachel discloses that she almost went to Europe with Chummy because "morals are like clothes and I'd scrapped one lot and hadn't found another to suit me." What William finally grasps is that it is not Chummy's morals to which Rachel objects, but to his manners—"It's these little remarks with an edge—you know, spiteful, cutting. He'd skin Patsey alive." William, with his sense of moral values, is non-plussed by Rachel's distinction between "being nasty and being simply immoral"; but he is flatly shocked by his aunt's angry reaction to his condemnation of Chummy. By repeating to himself that "values are relative," William is capable of accepting Rachel's substitution of manners for morals; but because he is incapable of going beyond moral relativity to a point where marriage and materialism become penultimate values, one "man of the family" is replaced by another.

The scope of the disinheritance, the extent of the separation from accepted social relationships and conventional moral values, has its degrees extending from the relatively mild dislocation felt by William to the nearly total isolation presented in "The Disinherited." In this story everyone either is or becomes "disinherited." Davina is a *déclassé* aristocrat, without money, reduced to exploiting her aunt's affection. "Something that should have occurred—she was not sure what—had not occurred yet, and became every day more unlikely"; and while she waits, she sells herself to Prothero for pocket money. Oliver, like Davina, is without a place in the social structure: "Oliver despised the rich and disliked the poor and drank to the bloody extinction of the middle classes." Prothero is psychologically disinherited. Having killed his mistress to escape the feeling of being "bought up," and having murdered again to lose his identity, Prothero claims to be "his own man." But nightly he is compelled to return to his writing table to exorcise his memory of Anita. His never finished interior monologue, where "the words sprang to their places with deadly complicity," with its hopeless and despairing postscript, reveals a mind enslaved to the very desire it so repeatedly denies.

Woven into the pattern of this social, moral, and psychological disorientation is the life of Marianne Harvey, whose story is an ironic reversal of the Cupid and Psyche tale. Marianne, who "looked like a diffident goddess" with "eyebrows turned up at her temples like impatient wings," half reluctantly, half compulsively, accompanies Davina to a party at Lord Thingummy's. In this "italianate palace" she meets more of Davina's *déclassé* friends and confronts her Cupid in the form of Oliver "with his dispirited viking air" who "longed to see himself otherwise, like any other man, with a sound and passionate core." In this rootless and disenchanted atmosphere where "the everyday became cloudy and meaningless and, like a tapestry, full of arrested movement," Marianne is seduced by a passionless and hollow Oliver in whom excitment took its most crippling form. When Marianne returns to the estate, "her serenity, mild good spirits and love of home" are gone—she forgets to change the water in the chrysanthemums, the dogs are not exercised. "Her faculty for disapproval seemed to be all used up," she cannot face her husband, "she was disoriented; she did not know."

Near the end of "The Disinherited" Davina, on one of her solitary walks, thinks: "One is empowered to live fully: occasion does not offer." Some of these sufferers of disorientation, like Prothero, are of course not "empowered to live fully"; while for some, like Davina and Marianne, the social structure, the established order, no longer provides them scope, "occasion does not offer." This relationship between the individual and the world outside himself to which he is attempting to adjust is never a static one. The emphasis, however, often falls on the fact that "occasion does not offer," especially when the established order which comprises the "occasion" is itself in a state of upheaval.

"Summer Night" is an exploration of the relation of the ego, the self, to a world in which values have been destroyed and the dependable patterns of social and familial relationships dislocated. As William Heath has pointed out, the entire story is played against the backdrop of the ultimate dislocation resulting from war. But the war *per se* is only one chaotic and destructive element among many in this story and they are all symbolized by the "summer night" which dominates the story from its opening at sunset to its bitter and dreamlike close at midnight.

In his conversation with Robinson, Justin Cavey, the impotent and tortured intellectual, says "Scrap 'me'; scrap my wretched identity and you'll bring to the open some bud of life. I *not* 'I'—I'd be the world." But as Justin discovers, the "I" dies hard; one's "wretched identity" cannot be scrapped, it can only be continually immolated in a world in which it cannot orient itself. Only Robinson, the uncontemplative man of action working at high pressure in his factory office or shooting off in his highpowered car, and Queenie, the deaf woman, "contemplative, wishless, almost without an 'I' " are capable of withstanding the forces of chaos from without and within.

Emma, "farouche, with her tentative little swagger and childish, pleading air of delinquency," succumbs to her sexual drives and under pretence of a visit leaves her husband and children to drive to a meeting with her lover, Robinson. She attempts to justify what she recognizes as an aberration of behavior by seeing it as a romantic adventure, a "pilgrimage"; but in Robinson's house of tile, chromium, and switches, she finds that his behavior is as mindless and mechanical as his factory and motorcar—"her adventure became the quiet practice with him." Emma's attempt to adjust her inner self to an act which will destroy all preexisting values and standards is crushed by Robinson's "stern, experienced delicacy." He forces her to see their meeting for what it is—"she thought for a minute he had broken her heart, and she knew now he had broken her fairytale."

The revelation of chaos and dislocation to which Aunt Fran is subjected is of a different but no less destructive kind. Always afraid of the "wakeful night" she eagerly awaits the barring and locking of the house, but, as she discovers, this does not prevent the shadow rising "up the cathedral tower, up the side of the pure hill." When she and her nephew, the major, hear noises from upstairs, Aunt Fran demands to go and see. Pushing open the door of Emma's bedroom, she finds Vivie, the carbon copy of her mother, bouncing on Emma's empty bed, her naked body covered with chalk pictures of snakes and stars, while "all her senses stood up wanting to run the night." Unlike Emma, Vivie is locked in, but this does not prevent her from stepping over the "one arbitrary line [which] divided this child from the animal."

Later, in her own room, Aunt Fran, "capable of no act . . . undone," feels that the war, the night, Vivie's nascent sexuality are all related:

> There are no more children: the children are born knowing. The shadow rises up the cathedral tower, up the side of the pure hill. There is not even the past: our memories share with us the infected zone; not a memory does not lead up to this. Each moment is everywhere, it holds the war in its crystal; there is no elsewhere, no other place. Not a benediction falls on this apart house of the Major; the enemy is within it, creeping about. Each heart here falls to the enemy.

The old aunt, "stranded here like some object on a spool that has run dry," finds that her values and standards, like Victorian morality, are anachronistic; she discovers that her "china kittens, palm crosses, three Japanese monkeys, *bambini,* Lincoln Imp, merry thought pen-wiper, [and] ivory spinning wheel from Cologne" are not enough to protect her in a world where even "our memories share with us the infected zone."

Justin Cavey, like Emma and Aunt Fran, is a victim of the "summer night." Locked in by the war, separated from the historical, cultural, intellectual traditions of a France, Germany, Italy which are no more, Justin retreats to the "impersonal, patient look of the thinker." His only defense is talk, but the casual inattentiveness of Robinson, and the "solitary and almost fairy-like world created by [his sister's] deafness" crush this defense and leave him "to face the screen of his own mind, on which the distortion of every one of his images, the war-broken towers of Europe, constantly stood." Justin's attraction to Robinson is nearly homosexual and certainly symptomatic of his relation to his dislocated world. Unable to adjust to the "fair, smiling, offhand, cold-minded man" or his mistress "crouching in her crouching car in the dark," Justin is reduced to the impotent action of writing Robinson a letter ending their friendship and condemning his "never failing imperviousness."

Queenie, Justin's deaf sister, is simultaneously the antithesis to and complement of Robinson. Unlike Robinson, Queenie, although deaf, is capable of intuiting subtle shifts in the emotional atmosphere and the "things she said out of nowhere, things with no surface context, were never quite off the mark." Yet "almost without an 'I'" she lives in a soundless world of her own, feeding on the memories of a single meeting with a lover in whose place she has, for this evening, substituted Robinson. Queenie is immured in her memories, Robinson in his imperviousness; as Justin puts it, "she does not hear with her ears, he does not hear with his mind." Neither of them sees any need for "a new form for thinking or feeling" for they are not aware of the destruction of the old.

While it might be argued that all of Elizabeth Bowen's short fiction deals with the relationship of innocence to experience, the complexity of that relationship should not be overlooked. The tension between the self and the world of external fact is, as Miss Bowen treats it, never simple or static. While her stories often depict a failure of synthesis or assimilation, the blame, if that word is appropriate, is never wholly to be placed at a single door. It is just as possible that the apparently objective and trustworthy world will betray the individual, as it is that the individual will fail to adjust to his world. The variations in thematic patterns of her short fiction suggest that cause, not verdict, is Elizabeth Bowen's concern. And if she most often turns her attention to failures, she does so in the interest of success.

RICHARD GILL

The Country House
in a Time of Troubles

Among contemporary writers in Ireland who lived through the "broken world" of the Troubles and their aftermath, it is Elizabeth Bowen who has the most memorably identified herself with the Big House. Throughout her fiction, from *The Last September* (1929) to *A World of Love* (1955), she has made the Anglo-Irish household a haunting setting and a vibrant symbol. And in *Bowen's Court* (1942), as well as in essays like "The Big House" (1942), she has also illuminated the complexities of its condition and fateful influence. Her abiding preoccupation with the great house entitles Elizabeth Bowen to a place not far from James, Yeats, and Waugh.

Like these others, Elizabeth Bowen comes to the house as both celebrant and critic. Indeed, as she reveals in autobiographical moments, her relationship with the house of tradition is at once more intimate and more ambivalent than theirs. James and Yeats bring to the house the susceptibilities and the detachment of the outsider; Miss Bowen speaks from within. The touchstone of her symbolism is Bowen's Court, the Italianate country house her ancestors built near Cork in the eighteenth century. From her summer visits there as a girl down through her occupancy as its mistress, she grew familiar with its customs and possessed by its moods. "The house," she has confided in *Bowen's Court*, "stamps its own character on all ways of living: I am ruled by a continuity that I cannot see." More inevitably than James or Yeats, she therefore turns to the great house as an emblem for a style of life. "As on a ship at sea," she remarks elsewhere, "there is a sense of

From *Happy Rural Seat: The English Country House and the Literary Imagination.*
© 1972 by Yale University. Yale University Press, 1972.

community"; and as if combining a Conradian feeling for its regimen with a Jamesian sense of its past, she continues: "This is, I suppose, the element of its spell. The indefinite ghosts of the past, of the dead who lived here and pursued the same routine of life in these walls add something, a sort of order, a reason for living, to every minute hour."

At the same time, however, Elizabeth Bowen ignores none of the incongruities involved with the great house—particularly one in Ireland. An Irish estate, she has admitted, is often "something between a *raison d'être* and a predicament." Considering Moore Hall, the family seat of the novelist, before it was burned down, she remarks that "while it stood, classic and bare and strong, the house embodied that perfect idea of living that, in actual living, cannot realize itself." And one reason for these disparities, as she recognizes because of her own background, is the historical position of the Anglo-Irish ruling class descending from Cromwellian forebears in relation to the natives of Ireland. "My family," she confesses, "got their position and drew their power from a situation that shows an inherent wrong." Paradoxically, therefore, the Big House may become a symbol of isolation as well as community. And in *Bowen's Court,* she dwells on just this peculiarity of Anglo-Irish households:

> Each of these family homes with its stables and farms and gardens deep in trees at the end of long avenues, is an island, a world. Sometimes for days together a family may not happen to leave its own demesne. . . . Each member of these isolated households is bound up not only in the sensation of living here. . . . Each of these houses with its intense, centripetal life is isolated by something much more lasting than the physical fact of space: the isolation is an affair of origin. It is possible that Anglo-Irish people, like other children, do not know how much they miss. Their existences, like those of other children, are singular, independent, and secretive.

Placing this emphasis on Bowen's Court, we must not, however, reduce her fiction to reportage: this would mistake her method and intention. In her own comments on setting in the novel she observes that fictitious places must "take on something from the at once simplifying and concentrated imagination which has created them—one may notice a sort of poverty in the atmosphere of a scene which the novelist has no more than 'copied.'" And there are undoubtedly literary influences at work as well. An admirer of Henry James, Elizabeth Bowen surely responded to the symbolic eminence of the country house in his work. With James, she has also shown a certain attachment to the more sophisticated branch of the Gothic tradition: the novelists of the nineteenth century, like Wilkie Collins and Sheridan Le Fanu, she has taken pains to note, saw "the possibilities of the country house from the point of view of drama, tension, and mystery." In her judgment, Collins wrings the last drop of effect from the forbidding mansion in *The Woman in White*; and Le Fanu's *Uncle Silas*, by dividing the scene between two houses—one civilized and comfortable, the other lugubrious—makes the contrast an element of the drama. Nonetheless, it is obviously Bowen's Court that remains paramount for her imagination. Speaking of what conditions the novelist, Miss Bowen has testified that for herself "the influence of environment is the most lasting" and "operated deepest down." And in her remarks on the relation of *Uncle Silas* to Le Fanu's Anglo-Irish experience, she might very well be referring to herself and providing a program note to several of her own novels:

> *Uncle Silas* has always struck me as being an Irish story transposed to an English setting. The hermetic solitude and the autocracy of the great country house, the demonic power of the family myth, fatalism, feudalism and the "ascendancy" outlook are accepted facts of life for the race of hybrids from which Le Fanu sprang. For the psychological background of *Uncle Silas* it was necessary for him to *invent* nothing. Rather, he was at once exploiting in art and exploring for its more terrible implications what would have been the norm for his heredity.

Certainly, the atmosphere herein described—the "psychological weather," to use Miss Bowen's own phrase—pervades *The Last September,* her novel about the predicament of the Anglo-Irish gentry during the Troubles. Danielstown, a lovely, lonely house—which the author admits derives from Bowen's Court—functions as both stage and symbol. The novel opens with Sir Richard and Lady Naylor, the owners of Danielstown, and their young niece Lois receiving guests on the steps outside; it closes with the house burning down after a raid. The phases of the action are marked off by the arrivals and departures of visitors, and throughout the novel the mansion, with its expressive rooms and brooding landscape, remains a constantly felt symbolic presence.

The tone of the novel is unusually ambiguous: while carrying on its familiar, comfortable routines, the house gives off an air of isolation, even unreality. The Naylors, trying to remain indifferent to the political conflict and violence in the sinister Ireland around them, keep up the conventions of hospitality and civilized form. But seated formally together at dinner, they and their guests seem, in contrast to the immutable family portraits above them, "unconvincingly painted, startled, transitory." In the evenings, the menacing sound of lorries and patrols just beyond the demesne intrudes upon the polite conversation on the terrace. This ambiguity is sharpest for young Lois. Despite herself, Lois lingers at Danielstown because she is struggling with her own personal sense of separateness, of adolescent exclusion from the world of adults. "I like to be in a pattern," she confides to her friend Marda. "I like to be related; to have to be what I am. Just to *be* is so intransitive, so lonely." On the surface, Danielstown seems to offer her the desired pattern, but Lois discovers there only the reflection of her own plight. Looking down at Danielstown from an enclosing mountain, she wonders why the occupants are not afraid:

> Their isolation became apparent. The house seemed to be pressing down low in apprehension, hiding its face, as though it had her vision of where it was. It seemed to huddle its trees close in fright and amazement at the wide light unloving country, the unwilling bosom whereon it was set.

And after every return, Lois feels that "she and these home surroundings still further penetrated each other mutually in the discovery of a lack."

The ambivalence of Lois, moreover, is not the only symptom of the uneasy tenor of life at Danielstown. Other characters display their own inadequacy, passivity, and frustration. One guest, Mr. Montmorency—an ineffectual man who might once have made a new life in Canada but never went—returns nostalgically to Danielstown for consolation. Ironically, he spends his time uxoriously combing his wife's hair and, later, entertaining an erotic fantasy about a departed guest. Lois's cousin Lawrence, an Oxford undergraduate, a materialist but moneyless, stays on for very practical reasons. "I have to eat somewhere," he admits. But he too is bored all the same: "I should like something else to happen, some crude intrusion of the actual. I feel all gassy from yawning. I should like to be here when this house burns." Young Gerald Lesworth, a pleasant English lieutenant garrisoned in Ireland, represents the "actual" and is, therefore, an "intrusion." Falling in love with Lois, he is callously humiliated by her aunt's inquiries about his financial and social eligibility and is finally made to realize that his feelings are not really returned. Consequently it is no accident that "his earthy vitality" is numbed by the glacial atmosphere of the drawingroom at Danielstown; or that his last, confused talk with Lois before his death takes place in the shadowed wood of the demesne, "where constricted by firs, thought and movement were difficult."

For all its loveliness, Danielstown is revealed as a world of divisions and separations—between the conventional and the actual, the accepted and the excluded, the private life and the political. Ironically, personal and historical destinies do finally meet in an act of violence: the house is burned down by the Irish rebels, and at the end we are told, "The door stood open hospitably upon a furnace."

It would be a mistake, however, to oversimplify *The Last September* as an indictment or a pathology, ironic and unsentimental as it is. There is no implication that the burning of Danielstown is in any way justified; indeed, its destroyers—described as "executioners bland from accomplished duty"— are also presented ironically. And the sentence quoted above—"The door stood open hospitably upon a furnace"—may be taken as having more than one prong. Although the imperceptions and disabilities of Danielstown are candidly considered, there lingers—as in the other Irish works mentioned above—an ungrudging sense of loss, of muted elegy. In a preface to a later edition of the novel, Elizabeth Bowen herself seems to be reminding the reader of this by calling attention to the title. "*The Last September*," she emphasizes, "takes its pitch from the month of the book's name." Certainly the novel is imbued with an autumnal vision of decline and decay; but September itself is Janus-faced, as the closing pages of the novel attest. "Every autumn," says a last visitor to Danielstown, "it strikes me this place really looks its best."

A novel of dispossession, *The Last September* never suggests that what has been destroyed did not represent certain values worth preserving. Indeed, in the other novels and short stories that Elizabeth Bowen published between the Troubles and World War II, the social and moral vacuum left by the destruction of the great house ironically brings it back to mind as an inviting image of community and order, embodying "that perfect idea of living that, in actual living, cannot realize itself." Though not always a major setting, the great house still remains an important reference point for orienting the reader to Miss Bowen's symbolic landscape; an off-stage thematic fulcrum, it serves—if only through allusion—to extend a meaning, accent an irony. In her first novel, *The Hotel* (1927), as Barbara Seward has noted, the family homestead has already been abandoned; but this does not grant its heroine, Sydney Warren, the kind of liberation young Lois anticipated in *The Last September,* for she comes to see her little English colony in Italy as unreal and weightless—governed not by any real attachment but by "some funny law of convenience." Again, in *To the North* (1932), the destruction of a great house becomes an elaborate metaphor for Cecilia Summer's state of grief and dislocation after the death of her husband.

In her later fiction, moreover, Elizabeth Bowen—rather like Forster and Waugh—finds her symbols of isolation and rootlessness in townhouses, city flats, provincial villas, and forlorn hotels—places which, divorced from any human past and suggesting only transience, call up the country house as counterfoil. In *The House in Paris* (1935), for example, the wealthy London home of Karen Michaelis and the *petit-bourgeois* establishment of Mme Fisher—one an impersonal museum, the other a forbidding jail—connote, as Sister Sharp observes, greater austerity and isolation than Danielstown ever did. In *The Death of the Heart* (1938), the servant Matchett says of the chilly London mansion of the Quaynes, "No, there's no past in this house," providing by indirection a contrast with the traditional country house and preparing the reader for the inhumanity of its residents toward the orphaned Portia. In the late short story "Ivy Gripped the Steps" (1945), an ostentatious villa by the seaside becomes the setting for the emotional betrayal of a small son of the poorer gentry.

Furthermore, this sense of the great house as an emblem of human community—implied but unaccented in the fiction that Elizabeth Bowen published between the wars—was poignantly sharpened by her experience of World War II. Living in London through the worst of the bombing, she witnessed the violence that had once swept away the world of Danielstown return with traumatic intensity. History had come full circle: there was greater need than ever for some perspective on the past, for some sustaining image of a viable future. Once more, Elizabeth Bowen returned to her roots: during the early part of the war, she wrote *Bowen's Court*, not to satisfy a nostalgic wish to escape into the past but to reappraise the significance of the landed tradition for the chaos of our time. "In my beginning is my end," she might have said—as did T. S. Eliot in "East Coker" (1940), a wartime poem motivated by much the same need and, incidentally, opening with the image of a house.

A labor of love, *Bowen's Court* belongs, from one point of view, with those other "biographies" of houses—*Earlham, Knole and the Sackvilles, Marianne Thornton*—which, characteristically produced by British novelists, nourish our social imagination by conjuring up a spirit of place and illuminating a style of life. From another point of view, it might well be associated with several English novels of the war period—*Between the Acts* (1941), *To Be a Pilgrim* (1942), *Brideshead Revisited* (1945)—which are informed by the same impulse to reassess the relation of the historic past to the contemporary world by focusing upon a country house. In any case, it is evident that Miss Bowen herself, while composing her chronicle, was explicitly working out themes that were later given fictional form in *The Heat of the Day* (1949), her own novel about wartime England. By her own account, the very paradox involved in writing about one house when all homes were threatened and many destroyed, provided illumination. "I have taken the attachment of people to places," she wrote in the book's afterword, "as being generic to human life, at a time when the attachment is to be dreaded as a possible source of too much pain. . . . But all this—the disparity or contrast between the time and the subject—has only acted to make it more important to me. I have tried to make it my means to approach a truth about life."

This truth involved, among other things, the recognition of both the perilous relationship between fantasy and action and the possibly salutary one between power and property. Her ancestors, Elizabeth Bowen perceives, often lived out their lives in subjection to some social or personal fantasy; and here she finds a parallel with the ideological conflicts of the present. "While I have studied fantasy in the Bowens," she observes,

> We have seen it impassion race after race. Fantasy is toxic: the private cruelty and the world war both started in the heated brain. Showing fantasy, in one form or another, do its unhappy work in the lives of my ancestors, I have been conscious at almost every moment of the nightmarish big analogues of today.

Her people, she goes on, were also infatuated with the idea of power; but here there is a difference between the past and the present. Her family and their associates, Miss Bowen maintains, were forced to practice a certain restraint because their power was mostly invested in property: "One may say that while property lasted the dangerous power-idea stayed, like a sword in its scabbard, fairly safely at rest. At least, property gave my people and people like them the means to exercise power in a direct, concrete and therefore limited way." Indeed, it is in the lack of property, she argues, that danger may lie, rather than in property itself:

> Without putting up any plea for property—unnecessary, for it is unlikely to be abolished—I submit that the power-loving temperament is more dangerous when it prefers or is forced to operate in what is materially a void. We have everything to dread from the dispossessed. In the area of ideas we already see more menacing dominations than the landlord exercised over land. The outsize will is not necessarily evil: it is a phenomenon. It

must have its outsize outlet, its big task. If the right scope is not
offered it, it must seize the wrong. We should be able to harness
this driving force: at present a minor society makes its own
major enemies.

The values with which Elizabeth Bowen set out, therefore, remained
constant—"accentuated rather than changed by the war."

In opposition to the nightmares of a material void, she places the "concrete and therefore limited" world of Bowen's Court. "Yes," she writes,
"here is the picture of peace—in the house, in the country round." Like all
pictures, she admits, it does not quite correspond to any reality; but in her
eyes this incongruity does not diminish the value of the Big House as a
symbol: "Bowen's Court was, in essence, a family home; since 1776 it had
been a symbolic hearth, a magnetic idea, the focus of generations of intense
living." Moreover, this idea, as she emphasizes elsewhere, is above all a
social idea—of good manners, good behavior, and easy, unsuspicious intercourse. In the Big House of the past, "society—or, more simply, the getting
together of people was meant at once to be a high pleasure and willing
discipline, not just an occasion for self-display." In the present, Miss Bowen
insists, the Big House still recalls the social idea to mind: " 'Can we not,' big
half-empty rooms seem to ask, 'be, as never before, sociable. Cannot we
scrap the past, with its bitterness and barriers, and all meet, throwing in
what we have?' "

That the writing of *Bowen's Court* strengthened Miss Bowen's feeling
for the great house as a symbol of community is further confirmed by *The
Heat of the Day*. In this novel about wartime England, two contrasting
houses symbolically extend the crisis in values dramatized by the love affair
between Stella Rodney, who has lost her position in the landed gentry
through divorce, and Robert Kelway, a lower middle-class Englishman,
whose susceptibility to fascism has turned him into a spy. One house is
Holme Dene, the pretentious, almost manorial suburban home of Robert
Kelway's family; the other, Mount Morris, the old country house in the
south of Ireland bequeathed to Stella's son Roderick by the cousin of his
dead father.

Holme Dene is, to use the phrase from *Bowen's Court,* "materially a
void." As Stella observes to herself on a visit, "You could not account for
this family by simply saying that it was middle class, because that left you
asking the middle of what? She saw the Kelways suspended in the middle of
nothing." This distinction between Stella and the Kelways, as William
Heath observes, is not a snobbish one: rather, it is meant to reveal that

Holme Dene is still another house of isolation—rootless, lifeless, empty of feeling. Though antique in appearance, the place is not actually old—even the oak beams are imitation. Its unsettled atmosphere and denial of emotional attachments are summed up in the fact that it is permanently up for sale and yet no one really minds. "Oh, but there will always be somewhere else," Robert asserts. "Everything can be shifted, lock, stock, and barrel . . . like touring scenery from a theatre." Significantly, Holme Dene is fatherless and husbandless; it has become the "projection" of Robert's mother, an incommunicative, obsessed woman, who rules over her domain like the evil spirit of a "bewitched wood." It is no accident, therefore, that when Robert attempts to justify his treason he should allude to Holme Dene. "I was born wounded; my father's son," he confides to Stella, "Unwhole. Never earthed in. . . . Not only nothing to hold, nothing to touch. No source of anything in anything."

Mount Morris, in contrast, gives Stella's son, a soldier in the war, something to hold, something to touch. Though he has never seen the house nor met the cousin who has left it to him, Mount Morris bestows on him the sense of community Robert Kelway so pathetically lacks:

> It established for him, and was adding to day by day, what might be called an historic future. The house came out to meet his growing capacity for attachment; all the more, perhaps, in that geographically standing outside the war it appeared to be standing also outside the present. The house, non-human, became the hub of his imaginary life.

To be sure, Mount Morris is involved with its own ironies: as the setting for the honeymoon of Roderick's parents, it was arguably inauspicious, since their marriage was broken by divorce; moreover, Stella, on her visit there as her son's emissary, recalls how Cousin Nettie, the last mistress, went mad within its walls. Nonetheless it becomes clear that Stella also comes to find in the house the hopeful possibility of renewal—through and for her son, if not herself. Her own generation, Stella admits, broke the link between the past and the future. However, "that her own life could be a chapter missing from this book need not mean that the story was at an end; at a pause it was, but perhaps a pause for the turning point?" Her dead cousin's "egotistic creative boldness" may have requisitioned Roderick for the future of Mount Morris; but the bequest also reveals to her a "man of faith." Roderick has not been victimized, Stella reflects in a passage that recalls the plight of Robert Kelway: "he had been fitted into a destiny; better, it seemed to her, than freedom in nothing."

This does not mean, of course, that Miss Bowen wishes to depict Mount Morris as a kind of Eden; what she implies rather is that the house may be the means of establishing some viable human order, "in a direct, concrete and therefore limited way." And here a comparison with *The Last September* may be instructive. In the early novel, young Lois, also seeking "pattern," eventually reacts against the confinement and isolation of Danielstown. In *The Heat of the Day,* Stella's son is no less aware that he has been made the object of "the unapprehendable wills of the dead." One winter night, on his first visit, the house summons him like a visionary presence:

> It could be that nature had withdrawn, leaving everything to be nothing but the identity of Mount Morris. The place had concentrated upon Roderick its being: this was the hour of the never-before—gone were virgin dreams with anything he had of himself in them, anything they had had of the picturesque, sweet, easy, strident. He was left possessed, oppressed, and in awe.

Yet it is also evident that the hard commitment demanded of him may involve, as his mother discerned, a better destiny than "freedom in nothing." While "followed by the sounds of his own footsteps over his own land," he contemplates, with an almost religious sense of transcendence, the kind of relation between the past and the future that the whole "idea of succession" inspires; and he then recognizes that, despite the impossibility of any final achievement, it is "a matter of continuing." After such a night, he is ready to accept the commonplace, practical tasks required to restore Mount Morris after the war—to nourish, as Eliot writes at the close of "The Dry Salvages," the "life of significant soil."

In *A World of Love,* her next novel after *The Heat of the Day,* Elizabeth Bowen, still preoccupied with the theme of continuity and renewal, made the Big House in Ireland the major setting and symbol as she did in *The Last September.* In fact, there are revealing correspondences and contrasts to be found between the early novel and the late one. Like Danielstown in *The Last September,* the house in *A World of Love* also suggests the inadequacies of a class but goes further by embodying its collapse. From the first page, the modest but once stylish mansion of Montefort is described as a decayed house—an emblem, like Gerontion's, for the listless condition of its older generation of inmates, who, as victims of their own "toxic fantasies," their own crippling fixations on the past, live on there in a kind of emotional limbo. It almost seems suggested that Montefort—with its moss, rust, felled trees, out-of-date calendars, defective clocks, and general "air of having gone down"—is what Danielstown might have become if it had survived, untended and unloved.

Even its proprietorship is ambiguous. The present occupants, Fred and Lilia Danby, do not possess Montefort; and they cannot really be called tenants or caretakers. Guy, its onetime owner, who died as a soldier in World War I, made no will, though engaged to Lilia. Montefort was therefore left to his cousin Antonia, who arranged a marriage between Lilia and Fred Danby and then allowed them to occupy it. Two daughters, Jane and Maud, are born of the marriage; but with the two women of the older generation still in love with the memory of Guy, the house remains gloomily oriented to the past, its people bound by animosity rather than affection.

Moreover, Jane, like young Lois in *The Last September,* is also on the threshold of life; but as the novel opens she seems less ready to cross over. Having grown up amid extreme situations and "frantic statements," she wishes an emotional equilibrium—with "no particular attitude toward the future" and only an "instinctive aversion to the past." In her eyes, Montefort is therefore neither a jail to escape from nor a haven to escape to: "The passions and politics of her family so much resembled those of the outside world that she made little distinction between the two."

For all this, however, Montefort does not suffer the fate of Danielstown. There is always the possibility of renewal. The affirmation evident in *The Heat of the Day* becomes, as Barbara Seward points out, considerably more pronounced in its successor. The "ghost" of Guy, called up by Jane's discovery of his love letters, is finally exorcised, bringing about a new orientation toward the future, not unlike Roderick's. Lilia and Fred find the hardness between them beginning to dissolve, and this provides them with a feeling of redemption: "Survival seemed more possible now, for having spoken to one another had been an act of love." The tolling of Big Ben over Maud's wireless restores the world of time to Montefort. Antonia herself looks to the future as the one thing left. And Jane goes forth to find her real lover exiting from a plane at a modern airport. Like its predecessor, *The Heat of the Day, A World of Love* affirms continuity through acceptance and adaptation through commitment. Again, the Big House survives.

HARRIET BLODGETT

The Necessary Child:
The House in Paris

The House in Paris (1935) is a subtle novel which Miss Bowen in 1948 identified as her favorite among her books, claiming also that it came to her with a special immediacy. Indeed, in no novel prior to this were her conceptions so fully translated into dramatic, aesthetically effective terms. Whatever may have been its emotional or subliminal genesis, *The House in Paris* is technically complex enough to suggest a careful working out of the initial imaginative apprehension. Returning to the three-part division and ten-year time lapse of *Friends and Relations,* now she smoothly interleaves the ten-year-old past (part 2) in the present (parts 1 and 2) so that a crucial past remains effectually alive in the present to support the book's structure of meaning. The Present, inevitably bearing the consequences of the Past, also redeems it. Although the tragic past terminated in disillusionment, sickness, and death, it has been balanced (part 2 is as long as parts 1 and 3 combined) against a hopeful present of growth and promise. Such configuration, which gives to the Past a destructive phase of the action and to the Present a constructive one, objectifies belief in the principle of redemptive renewal. But not just time serves. What *Friends and Relations* could not manage to say even with its blunt and prominent Jesse Tree, *The House in Paris* articulates by having the magical child of myths, an archetypal redeemer, effect the beneficent change that renews the Past and creates a Future.

The faith in a redemptive principle and belief in the whole nature of man, which pervade this novel and are particularly emphasized by its ending, are familiar enough. Miss Bowen may well say, "I imagine that if one

From *Patterns of Reality: Elizabeth Bowen's Novels.* © 1975 by Mouton & Co.

examined the works of any writer, a carry-over from one book to another would be found." She is a "next book" writer herself:

> The next book seems to promise to be the repository for everything I have not been able to say so far. Or, perhaps, that I have not been able to pin down. . . . All that remains with me of . . . [previous books] are the blunders—the ignorance that at the time prevented me gripping my subject as it ought to have been gripped, the imperfect realization of what I really did mean.
>
> What has been meant, but not yet properly said, still remains to be said . . . I am forever pinning my hopes on "my next book."

As a "next book," *The House in Paris* is distinctive as the first of her books in which faith in a redemptive principle is fully rendered because a symbolic redeemer appears onstage to help others. While she had not changed any of her earlier conceptions, with this book she had found her necessary symbol. Here first, and in every novel afterwards, the child-redeemer plays a central (if variable) role. The late fiction *Eva Trout* with its essentially "good" heroine who meets a violent death does not quite resemble the earlier *To the North* because of the complicating presence of Jeremy. Probably the fictional path Miss Bowen had been following of heroines reaching for wholeness of being was bound to lead her to *The House in Paris* as a next fiction. She did come upon an archetypal image for the Self in the child motif: "an image belonging to the whole human race and not merely to the individual" which, as Jung says, "expresses man's wholeness." The symbolic child "is all that is abandoned and exposed and at the same time divinely powerful; the insignificant, dubious beginning, and the triumphal end"; distinguishing itself "by deeds which point to the conquest of the dark." Miss Bowen herself suggests the inevitability of this particular book as her fifth novel: "*The House in Paris* . . . immediately took command of me and seemed to insist that I should write it."

With *The House in Paris,* Miss Bowen returns to a young heroine like Lois, but far more aggressive. The Past, Karen Michaelis's four months' long story, develops Karen's destructive revolt in search of herself. She does not come through her initiation into life's more bitter realities with distinction. A complicated twenty-three year old, she wants close personal relationships but is also narcissistically self-centered. "She looked at people at once vaguely and boldly; for years she had learnt from other eyes what hers did. This makes any lover or friend a narcissus pool; you do not want anyone else once you have learnt what you are; there is no more to learn." Daughter of a family which is only too representative of the sterility of ideas and feeling weakening the postwar upper middle class, Karen is both in and out of her environment—a "world she sometimes wished to escape from" but intends through her marriage to retain. Since part of her is loyal to the rational and social attitudes she has ingested, she has as a matter of course become engaged to the "right" sort of man (Ray Forrestier), for whom she has some affection. Either naïvely or self-deceptively willing to see marriage as a social matter, she has let herself discount deeper ties and strong passions. "She had not been born Karen Michaelis for nothing; it had been on the *daylight side* [italics mine] of marriage that she liked to dwell; she had expected, even, to show her friends that there is nothing in love to get so angry about." Meanwhile, she dreads the secure life she anticipates with Ray—"She had firm ground under her feet but the world shrank"—and such a profound sense of purposelessness drags at her that she must "not so much wonder why she was here as why she was ever anywhere." "Ray" has been given his particular name by Miss Bowen in order to emphasize the "light" or more rational and more conscious love tie—human and divine. "Karen," who withholds her emotional self from Ray, is a *Koré* who has an unstated (but very clearly implied) religious problem. She is not so much another Janet or Laurel as another disaffected Lois or Sydney who cannot acknowledge a deep identification with deity; or, in mythic terms, "marry" herself to God or His purposes. The Michaelis world gives only superficial assent to anything. In fact she has been born Karen Michaelis "for nothing," "for nothing." The phrase, in ironic repetitions, rings through the book.

In a general way, Karen recognizes what she actually wants: to fulfill her emotional capacities, to satisfy some passionate imperative dictated by her own being; "If one begins to think, why should one ever do anything? Marry most of all. . . . I don't want to do something that a reason's been found for; I want to do something I must do." What could be the basis for the ultimate surrender of self becomes the basis for an illicit love affair with Max Ebhart, disastrous in its consequences. Karen's attempt to complete herself through this passion is also an attempt to free herself from her family and, broadly, to impose herself on life by challenging it dangerously. She wants to feel a sense of "power" over her existence. When, however, she is herself challenged by life, she crumples, repudiating her child, eschewing love, settling into an unsatisfactory marriage with Ray, seeing "nothing but failures." "If revolutions do not fail, they fail you," Karen at one point observes. She then goes on to fail her own.

The narrow house in Paris, the junction point where Karen first met Max and where he afterwards died, is the principal setting for the events, ten years later, of the Present, compact within half a day. Appropriately, the half-day which is to effect a transition between a moribund past and a freed future extends from dawn to dusk, transitional points in a day (it also begins and ends at railway stations). In this somber house haunted by past tensions, where live old Mme Fisher, bed-ridden since the shock of Max's suicide, and her spinster daughter Naomi, once Max's fiancée, nine-year-old Leopold waits nervously. The son of Karen and the Jew, he has been brought from his adoptive parents in Italy to meet Karen for the first time (i.e., the part-Jew found a home in Italy, where his favorite city is Rome). By chance Leopold shares his important day with eleven-year-old Henrietta Mountjoy, an innocent waiting here between trains on her way to her grandmother's at Mentone. Through the two children a second and more successful initiation theme is developed. Karen's failure to appear subjects Leopold to shock, effecting a structural parallelism between past and present. But the resilient child survives his crisis and is only more determined to have his rightful heritage. Ray, who arrives in Karen's stead, courageously resolves to bring Leopold to her; and the novel ends anticipating a viable existence in the future of its characters.

Imaging Ray and Leopold as heroes, the book concludes on a very strong positive note:

> Egotism and panic, knowing mistrust of what was to be, died in Ray as he waited beside Leopold for their taxi to come: the child commanded tonight, I have acted on his scale.
>
> Here, at the head of the ramp, they stood at a commanding, heroic height above the level of Paris, which they saw. Leopold said: "Is it illuminated?" The copper-dark night sky went glassy over the city crowned with signs and starting alight with windows, the wet square like a lake at the foot of the station ramp.

The terms of the affirmation are significant. Miss Bowen constructs her own metaphor out of the sobriquet for Paris, the City of Light. Leopold's query (as if he recalls St. Peter's in his beloved Rome) brings an immediate response: a light on darkness. The vault of heaven is illuminated over a city "crowned with signs" as the lights come on in human dwellings. It is as if someone has given a sign that life is illuminated even as man is illuminated—Miss Bowen's book itself has, indeed, given such a sign. Her novel about growth subtends a pattern of meaning: there is a superior capacity in man and so light can succeed to dark. He may mature into light, or, suddenly "starting alight," he may see it through an immediate, intuitive perception of a "sign," a symbol. Maturation into light obviously bespeaks a particular ethos on this novel's part: light is right reason, not intellect. The child for all his immaturity, then, remains a vessel of light: he is closer to the source of being, even analogous to the Christ hero. It behooves the adult to retain the glow of the child he once was, as the Wordsworthian *Little Girls* also insists. The reader remarks the "little child shall lead" effect here: "The child commanded tonight, I have acted on his scale." He also remarks the perspective. The heroic quest for self necessitates a journey into and an acceptance of the total self: the point is imaged by the cap-a-pie elements in the final figure whereby we are caused to stand at the heroic heights but meanwhile regard the "lake" (cf. Markie's dislike of lakes in *To the North*) at the foot of the ramp. The final figure is a terse reminder that the head must include the foot, that the commanding height is not achieved without the lake of the unconscious and irrational which is the source of the conscious and the locus of the Self. Whether chance or fortunate choice led her, Miss Bowen embeds in her final image of a city "crowned with signs" a mandala, a geometric pattern of wholeness, of the circle squared: "the wet square like a lake." In the waters of the "lake" lie faith as well as evil; and by such waters the imagination—of writer and of reader—may be fecundated.

Avoiding an abrupt, interrupting flashback, Miss Bowen obliquely insinuates the Past into the narrative present by providing it contexts. The story of Karen (to be narrated rather than recalled in first person) is suggested, for one, as being the account Karen gave Leopold "in the course of that meeting that never happened, that meeting whose scene remained inside Leopold": The Past ostensibly is Leopold's interior projection of her account. Since Leopold assumed that, upon coming, Karen would communicate perfectly with him, a cryptic allusion to her memory, could (or would) she command it perfectly, follows the assigning of "scene" to Leopold's interior:

> You suppose the spools of negative that are memory (from moments when the whole being was, unknowing, exposed), developed without being cut for a false reason: entire letters, dialogues which, once spoken, remain spoken for ever being unwound from the dark, word by word.
> This is, in effect, what she would have had to say.

No experiences or acts, in short, can ever be negated: the sensibility retains them; life retains them. They can only be denied. That Karen's memory is being invoked for the Past is supported dramatically once during her account, through a tense shift which, by becoming present, conveys the fact that Karen still remembers especially the rain at Hythe where she consummated her love:

> Not having been here before and now coming with Max made an island of the town. It stayed like nowhere, near nowhere, cut off

> from everywhere else. Karen cannot divide the streets from the patter of rain and rush of rain in the gutters. She remembers a town with no wind, where standing on the canal bridge you hear trees sighing with rain. . . . All Saturday night, rain rustled the chestnut across the street.

This was the time of the Great Rain in Karen's own creation myth, when she stepped out of her own frame or context and into a different picture of life, an abrupt, and (to her) disastrous change not to be forgotten. The idea that we are in Leopold's consciousness will also be picked up only once during the Past, when he is addressed directly: "Having done as she knew she must, she did not think there would be a child: all the same, the idea of you, Leopold, began to be present with her." A significant moment has been chosen for this direct address. Conceiving the idea of Leopold is immediately accompanied for Karen by the "shock of tenderness and life opening." Karen not only conceives, but conceives of Leopold as a renewing force, as is to become his willing role in the Present. Furthermore, having *grasped* him, she can never truly be severed from him, a truth Leopold grasps with no difficulty at all.

In addition to being her recall to Leopold during their non-meeting, the full story of Karen is also proposed as a possibility of art, if not of "real life." Leopold naïvely imagined that perfect true discourse between human beings was possible; "actually, the meeting he had projected could take place only in Heaven—call it Heaven; on the plane of potential not merely likely behaviour. Or call it art, with truth and imagination informing every word. Only there—in heaven or art, in that nowhere, on that plane—could Karen have told Leopold what had really been." It bears repeating that Miss Bowen has no such Platonic mistrust of the artist-liar as William Heath claims. She reminds us that her novel offers the more nearly perfect reality of art; "collects round it real-er emotion than a real act" [in *Eva Trout*]. On the novel's plane, clock time like other limitations may be abrogated. Time ceases during the flashback: part 1 concludes, as part 3 resumes, with the suspended statement "Your mother is not coming; she cannot come." No time, thus, has elapsed while the Past explained Karen's non-appearance. Time advances only in the Present. Actually, because of the novel's construction, Past and Present coexist in the aesthetic experience. Since response to the Past includes anterior response to the Present, it must be more complex. Knowing the price of Karen's revolt—the homelessness of Leopold, the attrition of life in Paris—insures objective distance: sentimentally sympathetic identification with Karen is impossible. Conversely, Leopold predisposes us towards Karen: to sharing his powerful faith in her and believing what he assumes—that there must be point to her behavior, meaningful answer to his "Why am I?

What made me be?" We return to a Present (3) modified because it coexists with and yet advances from, transcends, the Past. Our experience of the whole novel, then, is one of human actions shaped to meaning. Art, informed by "truth and imagination," has shown that life can be redeemed.

What immediately caused Leopold was Karen's desire for new life. In the sterile Michaelis world of part 2 there is adequate cause for Karen's revolt. Miss Bowen damns with faint praise Karen's "charming family," only too representative of "the class that in England changes least of all"—arid in its ideas, isolated in its identifications, self-protective and restrictive in its values:

> The Michaelis lived like a family in a pre-war novel in one of the tall, cream houses in Chester Terrace, Regent's Park. Their relatives and old friends, as nice as they were themselves, were rooted in the same soil. Her parents saw little reason to renew their ideas, which had lately been ahead of their time and were still not out of date. Karen had grown up in a world of grace and intelligence, in which the Boer War, the War and other fatigues and disasters had been so many opportunities to behave well. The Michaelis's goodness of heart had a wide field: they were not only good to the poor but kind to the common, tolerant of the intolerant.
>
> In her parents' world, change looked like catastrophe, a thing to put a good face on: change meant nothing but loss. To alter was to decline. . . . If change did break in, you bowed and accepted it.

Neither the seasons nor the passions can impinge on the Michaelises:

> Pattering spring showers brought the trees right out; the last leaves cast their sheaths; thundery light, toppling ink-purple clouds across the ends of streets made the green burn. The suburbs tossed with lilacs and red may. Between thunder and sun, the Nash terraces round the Regent's Park, the trees in their May haze, took on their most theatrical air—but indoors at Chester Terrace, Michaelis family life continued as ever: intelligent, kind, calm.

Early in her account Karen will express a half-serious "wish the Revolution would come soon; I should like to start fresh while I am still young, with everything that I had to depend on gone. I sometimes think it is people like us . . . people of consequence, who are unfortunate: we having nothing ahead." To escape a world where "*They* keep me away from everything that has power," Karen constructs her own revolution through Max.

The symbolic solitary journey during which an initiate learns the nature of death begins Karen's cycle of change. After she has with mixed feelings become engaged to Ray, she flees from everyone's congratulations to visit "the most unconscious of her relations," her Aunt Violet in Ireland. Because Violet is slowly dying the visit reverberates through the novel. No one close to Karen has yet died. Violet's impending death therefore shocks Karen profoundly; it presages her own death. While Miss Bowen does spare Karen the crudity of a trip to the graveyard like Sydney's eight years earlier, she is subjecting Karen to the same emotional experience of mortality that makes the waste of one's days seem unendurable. The fatalistic peace of pastoral Rushbrook, where all the "ticking clocks did little to time" except mark it, is repellent "to something proud and restless—the spirit perhaps—that looked out from inside." When Violet acknowledges her sense of a life imperfectly fulfilled, what can Karen think of her own days?—"Could she have wished to be trodden down in a riot, be a mark for anger or go down on a helpless abandoned ship? Her life here was very much confined, for she must on no account walk uphill. Did she ever think, 'Well, what if I walk uphill?' " The youthfulness of the wishes betrays their true referent; their tenor bodes change. Karen herself wants to suffer danger and dare risks; to escape confinement and face life heroically. Karen (as her son Leopold is later to do) sees herself as a hero, a major step in the emergence of individual entity. Soon Max will empower a symbolic act of defiance lest she be "left to die like Aunt Violet." Now, however, Karen can do no more than leave the agitating waters of "Rushbrook" with their premonitions of death, although it was "useless to wish she had never come to Mount Iris; the cold zone crept forward everywhere."

Actually Karen's journey of transformation has begun with her lonely pilgrimage to Aunt Violet's purple mountain of death, but Miss Bowen's mythic methods become overt only upon Karen's departure from Ireland. Traditionally a journey over water has served as symbol for passage from one phase of existence to another; Karen's journey across the Irish Sea, however, is more precisely identified: hers is a night journey far downward for which she is provided with a guide who betokens the sensuality which Karen is to experience upon returning to England. Appropriate rituals are performed before Karen's crossing; a sop is fed to Cerberus so that the underworld may be attempted:

> Someone soon to start on a journey is always a little holy, so
> Karen was allowed to stay outside the talk. . . . Beside Uncle Bill,
> a visitor's dog sat up to beg politely; he, frowning carefully,

dropped a tea-cake into its mouth.

He said: "Don't worry," three times.

Karen's voyage to Fishguard is superintended by a figure named only Yellow Hat, an earthy Irish girl who attaches herself to Karen on the boat. She is aptly enough associated with hats (cf. *A World of Love*), because they are depth symbols for personality changes. Yellow Hat, who takes her pleasures easily, without Karen's finicky distinctions, is also a speaker of portentous words:

> Karen said: "Any terrors I've ever met have always been rather dull."
>
> "Ah, but," said her friend astutely, "perhaps *your* poison's not mine!"
>
> "I don't know what my poison is," said Karen, smiling.
>
> "Then beware, as the gyspy said!" exclaimed Yellow Hat. Her big silly face took on that immortal look people's faces have when they say more than they mean.

Yellow Hat is an aspect of Karen herself. If she is not one that Karen can yet consciously acknowledge, the process of change has nonetheless begun: "Meeting people unlike oneself does not not enlarge one's outlook; it only confirms one's idea that one is unique. All the same, in the confusion of such encounters, things with a meaning ring, that grow in memory later, get said somehow—one never knows by whom." "Your poison's not mine," Karen herself says—to Naomi (at this time Max's fiancée) soon after reaching England; and to herself, after Max. There will be no heroic ascent for Karen, and no more contrivedly symbolic scenes like the Yellow Hat one in her story. Yet a mythic going-down anticipates a coming-up. The mythic Return is to be enacted only during the last portion of the novel, with the heroic image of Ray and Leopold as its climax.

Karen first met Mme Fisher's protégé Max when at eighteen she was a boarder at Mme Fisher's; and "every movement he made, every word she heard him speak left its mark on her nerves." But she came back to England: "she grew up, her regard for order overtook her sensation"; the "rule of 'niceness'" resumed in her life; she forgot him. Significantly, however, when Naomi (in England with Max on business) urges Karen to a reunion, Karen tries to defer it until after both she and Naomi are married. The reunion, unavoidable, is decisive for Karen: "Max put his hand on Karen's, pressing it into the grass. Their unexploring, consenting touch lasted; they did not look at each other or at their hands. When their hands had drawn slowly apart, they both watched the flattened grass beginning to spring up again, blade by blade." The image of grass which resists their imprint is to recur to Karen often, signifying to her variously that Naomi need not know about them, and that they can have no permanence together, and—a more positive conception—that Max offers her a means to conquer death: the grass restores itself. A tense confrontation at a crowded railway station when Karen comes to see Max and Naomi off to Paris commits Karen to her revolution through Max. The time is May Day, associable traditionally with fertility rituals, but also, more contemporaneously, with class revolt; a fact picked up by a metaphor of "stout men agitating from carriage to carriage" who "bore down on Karen and Max" so that "there was no escape" from each other. Within a few weeks, Karen will envision herself fighting behind street barricades. Upon the news, some time later in May, of Violet's death, Karen "saw the dug-up daisies on the lawn at Rushbrook, the death had been then. She saw the strong grass at Twickenham springing up after her and Max's hands." She is ready for her affair with Max.

After their assignation at Hythe, Karen explains to Max that she came largely out of reaction to her life: "I found I was in a prison—no, locked into a museum full of things I once liked, with nothing to do now but look at them and wonder why I had." But her post-coital stream of consciousness more completely reveals both what impelled her and what will induce her later collapse. When Karen returns to consciousness and the "idea" of Leopold begins "to be present" in her, she has her one gratifying moment, since she now feels the "shock of tenderness and life opening"; otherwise, her thoughts are less sanguine. The resumption of her self-conscious identity in the world of time carries a sense of doom; for "While it is still Before, Afterwards has no power, but afterwards it is the kingdom, the power and the glory. You do not ask yourself, what am I doing? You know. What you do ask yourself, what have I done? You will never know." Her now incomprehensible, definitive act appalls her. She cannot comfort herself that it has "been escape": "Were you not far out, is there no far out, or is there no current there? I am let back, safe, too safe; no one will ever know. What they never know will soon never have been. I shall die like Aunt Violet wondering what else there was; from this there is no escape for me after all." Without the consequence of detection, her rebellion against the void of Michaelisdom will have failed, but apparently "One hopes too much of destroying things. If revolutions do not fail, they fail you." Her symbolic conquest of death has failed: "This seemed to have to be. . . . It looked like the end. I did not see it would have an end. . . . The grass sprang up when we took our hands away. . . . I thought tonight would be the hour of my death but here I still am, left to die like Aunt Violet after mother has died like her." Karen cannot bear the fact that now "nothing more has to be." The theme of consequences (both result and retribution) strengthens. Were there a child, there would be "something to dread," detection; but, more important, a child would give her passion real identity: "I should see the hour in the child. I should not have rushed on to nothing. He would be the mark our hands did not leave on the grass. . . . I could bear us both lying tired and cast-off if it were for him, if we were his purpose." To create, not merely to destroy, is what Karen desires; to be the agent, not merely the victim, of life force. A child would give point and continuity to her days so that "they would not fall apart," would not have been "for nothing." But he would be a "disaster" to her family, who "would not know where to turn to save me for themselves."

The thought of her family stimulates a fear dream in which she is putting on her clothes (resuming a former self-concept) to return home in, and they are disagreeably wet and terrifyingly adhesive. Karen cannot deny her fear at having sinned and so exposed herself to judgment. Part of Karen yearns to regress to the safety of childhood:

> Not her hiddenness now but her unhiddenness made her heart thump chokingly, as it did years ago when, playing hide and seek, she heard the steps of the seekers go by just the other side of the curtain, or heard them come into the dark room where she hid. The curtain would fall, the light would discover her before she could slip out to bolt for "home," which used to be by the gong, at the foot of the stairs. Once you were "home" you won, you could not be caught. So sometimes you struck the gong.

Although because fear conflicts with desire the revolutionary theme returns—to be "caught" by Max, to have a child—fear is stronger. Karen reassures herself that she will be safely undetected, for "No one will ever know. . . . He will never be born to be my enemy. . . . Once "home" you are safe . . . no one knows where you were hiding." Fear is very strong, but the dark room, memory, has stronger influence yet. From herself Karen will never be able to hide her "exposure"—though she may in after years attempt to suppress conscious recognition and accompanying guilt.

Karen's future emotional condition is predicted by her monologue with its burden of guilty fear. She is more disturbed than gratified by her actions, for all that she was impelled by spiritual aspiration to be a true entity, not merely by carnal urge. Granted she has some strength in pursuing self-definition, she is not single-minded about it. She will face up poorly, then, to the double surprise shocks of Max's suicide and the unexpected (miraculous) pregnancy—"having done as she knew she must she did not think there would be child." Ironically, had Max not died, she might have survived her disturbing sexual initiation, for it belatedly brings her a sense of fulfillment. Although Karen does not come to Hythe out of love, even assumes, in fact, Max's not really loving her, she wants and does gain his love. On Sunday her relationship with Max passes into a new phase:

> Last night seemed to be undone, so that they kissed with unfamiliar gentleness, tasting rain on each other's lips. Drawing apart like a pair of very young people, they stared at each other, and at what had happened now. Her heart stood still, as when she first thought of Leopold: she felt the same shock of tenderness and life opening. The face she found was the face she had failed to find on the dark pillow. This beginning of love, wanting new hands, lips and eyes, made them stand apart patiently looking at the trodden grass between them.

The rain they taste on each other's lips is the fructifying rain of vegetation myth; not the rain of "disaster" but the freshening grace of love. Something capable of permanence has finally been effected—they have at last marked the grass—and something has been renewed in Karen because life has opened into love.

Thus strengthened within, Karen reenters Michaelisdom—where no one will ever *know*—to confront its defensive system, the weaponry used to counter a "dread of chaos" which is the class heritage. Mrs. Michaelis hides her knowledge that Karen was not, as she claimed, spending the weekend with a girlfriend, conducting "a savage battle for peace" in a "deadly intention to not know" where Karen actually was. "Karen saw what was ruthless inside her mother." The narrator carefully juxtaposes refusal to know about Karen with refusal to countenance overt grief over Violet (the decorum of the Michaelis household has been evident ever since the first news about Violet came: "Mrs. Michaelis had not wept for years, and never in the drawingroom; she could not begin now"). The refusal to admit feelings honestly and to share them is part of a larger refusal to face existence squarely. The Michaelis world dares not acknowledge turbulence beneath the surface lest the surface become dangerously agitated too. Karen rashly queries how much her mother minds about Violet and the response she gets is the impersonal one of someone for whom poise has taken on almost an absolute value:

Mrs. Michaelis sat nobly in the armchair, eyes fixed on the second page of *The Spectator,* behaving as she had behaved in August 1914. She said with unshaken innocent simplicity: "It is the idea of her not being there, I suppose."

She dares not look up and say: "You transgress," though she feels that; she won't ask why I ask. Her resistance is terrifying; she would rather feel me almost hate her than speak. The good morale of our troops won the war.

Now Karen sees, as she had not seen before, that her mother is saving herself at the expense of Karen; that "when mother does not speak [about where I've been] it is not pity or kindness; it is worldliness beginning so deep down that it seems to be the heart." Mrs. Michaelis herself belatedly admits that she should have shown "more courage," but Karen never respects her again.

Although Karen refuses to renounce Max, she is not destined to enjoy her love since he slashes his wrists in the Fisher house upon returning to Paris. He marks with blood the house which killed his manhood: the trail of his blood extends from the hearth of the deadly Mme Fisher to her doorstep but leaves no stain in the street, where he dies. The twisted relationship between Max and Mme Fisher (reported rather than dramatically realized) is a disquieting example of female destructiveness. Mme Fisher is a creature of formidable will—"all mind and will," her daughter says. Originally, Karen is attracted to the force in Mme Fisher, her power to wrench life her own way, and dispassionately admires Mme Fisher's skill at manipulating people; but once Karen is involved with Max, she increasingly fears her. Through her energy, the force of her mind and will, Mme Fisher (metaphorically, the intermittent lighthouse) has disharmonized Max's personality: "The sea crept on the shingle with a half-living rustle; on its far-out silence Dungeness lighthouse flashed, stopped, flashed. . . . She [Mme Fisher] can never have wanted Max to be quiet; when he's quiet he's not hers. He was hers tonight when we saw the lighthouse, hers when we came in. . . . I have been frightened ever since I stood with Max on the front and saw the lighthouse out there, that night." Max himself explains that "as she saw me, I became. Her sex is all in her head, but she is not a woman for nothing. . . . Women I knew were as she made me see them: they were not much. Any loves I enjoyed stayed inside her scope; she knew of them all. She mocked and played on my sensuality."

Mme Fisher, who imposed her will on Max, succeeded in weakening his masculinity as a center of energy and purpose. Her pernicious effect as an incarnation of the malign *Magna Mater* is evident in Max's relations with women. He decided to marry Naomi, not for love or for passion, but as "someone to make for me an unattackable safe place"; passive, gentle Naomi is "like furniture or the dark." His falling in love with Karen, with whom he might have had a less dependent and deceptive relationship, is initially more promising. But since Mme Fisher has corroded his confidence in himself and in life, Max has no faith in this love. We learn from Naomi's account of his final moments that he "began to attack his own nature. 'What she [Karen] and I are,' he said, 'is outside life; we shall fail: we cannot live what we are.'" His suicide itself occurs when Max discovers how much Mme Fisher wants him to marry Karen: he has no independent existence; he has merely confirmed her desires when he thought he was finally acting for himself. His suicide, an impulsive "passionate" act, is at once a despairing acknowledgment that he cannot escape her and a protest against her unholy dominion. Part of the truth is apprehended by Naomi, who, "saw then that Max did not belong to himself. He could do nothing that she had not expected; my mother was at the root of him. I saw that what she had learnt about you and him pleased her, that she had pleasure in it in some terrible way." But Mme Fisher knows the rest: "It was commendation he could not bear. I was commending him when he took his knife out. He struck myself, himself, my knowledge of him." Ambitious for Max (Karen is wealthy), respecting strong personalities (Karen is forceful), Mme Fisher saw Karen, not Naomi, as a worthy successor. But power which "overreached itself" instead broke the man she meant to save.

Max's death settles Leopold's fate. Left to face her unexpected pregnancy without Max, Karen is not so brave anymore. For quite conventional reasons, to avoid the awkwardnesses attending illegitimacy, she plans to give up her child:

> "I could go off and live with him somewhere, I suppose. Somewhere where no one knew us—I cannot even imagine such a place. But if he is like Max and me he would hate that—hate exile, hate being nowhere, hate being unexplained, hate having no place of his own. Hate me too, because of all that. He would be better without me, in any place he could believe was his."

Besides implying self-dislike, Karen's fear that he will "hate" her betrays a questionable self-concern. Miss Bowen, who directs her novel's action so that it reunites mother and child, would say that Karen belongs with her child. When Karen herself instigates a reunion with Leopold after ten years, one may take it as an indication that Karen is beginning to grow again. Her inability to come points to unresolved conflicts, but Leopold's aggressive determination to be loved is so strong that one anticipates he will help her transcend them. If Leopold can make Karen assume her moral responsibility to him, if Leopold can restore Karen to living at harmony with her total self, patterns will have been completed. Leopold will be the redemptive symbol he was originally "conceived" to be, and Karen will have made the crossing to "Fishguard" (to greater life; the name chosen for the symbolic association of "fish" with spiritual regeneration) she only began by descending with Yellow Hat.

Leaving the past before Leopold is born, we learn in the present (part 3) and principally through Ray, of Leopold's birth and Karen's subsequent marriage. The marriage is a stagnancy in which neither partner effectively assimilates the past, Ray's unusual willingness to adopt Leopold merely strengthening Karen's rejection of her child. Mme Fisher's claim that Karen has a "dread" of the past is confirmed by Ray's recall of Karen's words. She dreads Leopold because he has become a personal, negative symbol which has accreted all the emotional energies she once expended: he is anticipation and disappointment, pride and sense of failure, and certainly guilt, rather than simply a child: " 'You don't know,' she had said. 'He is more than a little boy. He is Leopold. You don't know what he is.' " Not only would he force her to love. Leopold is the "enemy" who would force her to remember what she would forget. Karen betrays her desire to abrogate the past in wanting to return to her original relationship with Ray, insisting that her experience with Max has in no way altered her: "Why should what happened to me change you? It should be me that has changed, but I stay the same: you have changed. . . . I want to be back where we started." Leopold also symbolizes Karen's unresolved relationship with Ray, and for both her and Ray, in fact. Until the day Ray meets Leopold, for Ray too he is no real child: "His intense feeling for Leopold had used his inner energy, without letting, all these years, any picture form. Out of known and unknown he had not tried to compound the child. 'Our child would have lived if you'd wanted him,' she said once. 'But you wanted your own ideas more. All you wanted was Leopold.' " Hysterical though Karen's accusation may sound, it is not without basis or thematic point: Ray's Leopold-obsession has made their marriage too sick to bear life. When Ray does finally acknowledge Leopold to be perceivable as a real child and admit that all these past years, "he did not know; she was right," it is a quietly underplayed, but very important, moment of growth.

We get some sense of what Leopold may have represented to Ray from his recall of the "unspoken dialogue": a debate epitomizing the tensions of his and Karen's union. In this colloquy, in contrast to his self-awareness at the house in Paris, Ray responds to Karen's accusation "Simply a child! He is more to you than that" with a complacent, "Well, if he is?" Karen objects that Ray's kind of love is an emotional parasitism: "You feed your complicated emotion on what happened to me." The pith of her accusation is that her experiences gratify him by affording him the enjoyment of his own goodness: "No, what you remember is taking me back. Kissing me with that unborn child there. That emotion you had." Ray does not agree with all Karen says, but neither do his complacent responses succeed in contradicting what she means and objects to—her feeling that to him she is not just herself, Karen whom he loves, but rather, Karen-to-forgive:

> HE If I have [changed], it is in loving you more than I did.
> SHE Because Max loved me?
> HE That may be.
> SHE Because I loved Max.
> HE That may be, too.

Despite the bravado, Karen really does not forgive herself for having loved Max as she did. And not only does she fear that Ray prefers to see her as an object of forgiveness; she fears that Ray actually does not forgive her for preferring Max to him. We briefly enter Karen's consciousness:

> When she thought, she thought: Forgiveness should be an act,
> but this is a state with him. So he has not forgiven. He forgives
> me for wanting Max while there is my not wanting Leopold not
> to forgive me for. If I gave in to wanting Leopold, Ray would
> bring Max back. He won't let us be alone. He does not forgive.

Karen may well be right about the transference; Ray has never faced up to the problem of Max. The "idea" of Leopold is the idea of Ray: Ray's self-concept as a good, forgiving man. Forgiveness should be a completed act, not an activity. For Ray to come for Leopold today is a decisive action to consummate forgiveness and advance from it.

It is easier to imagine oneself taking another man's child than to take him. Also, Ray has never been forced before to confront and surmount any resentments toward Max. Today Ray faces the unpleasant reality of Leopold and his own anti-Max self; and "no one could be less merely impish than Leopold. Behind the childish *méchanceté*, Ray saw grown-up avengingness pick up what arms it could . . . Karen's unalarmed smile appeared on Leopold's lips when he had said this, but his deliberate look was from someone else's eyes. Ray saw for the moment what he was up against: the force of a foreign cold personality." Acknowledging the objective reality of Leopold, Ray accepts him. Taking him converts Ray's sentimental charitableness towards Leopold—an easy willingness to do good, sustained without confrontation of its object—to real charity. In Ray's self-exertion and growth and the promise of a better marriage, the Present has effected good. But the beneficial aspects of the Present extend beyond Ray. The Present belongs also and very importantly to the children.

BARBARA BELLOW WATSON

Variations on an Enigma:
Elizabeth Bowen's War Novel

In a comment on her wartime short stories, Elizabeth Bowen says, "I see war . . . more as a territory than as a page of history." This territory is the setting of her first postwar novel, *The Heat of the Day,* a war novel without the blood, brutality, boredom, and obsessive physicality of other war novels. Bowen's territory of war is a place of blind darkness except for apocalyptic moments of blinding light, a place in which language keeps closing up, like yesterday's code, against communication, a place in which windows give no view, mirrors do not reflect truly, and pictures are not worth any more than words, since they too falsify. In this territory, sanity and madness interpenetrate, opponents and opposites are twinned. All questions take an epistemological edge, small ones as well as large. If war is perceived in a new way, that is only partly because the author is a woman and a highly individual observer. The reason is also that the nature of war itself has changed.

The single heavy line drawn across history by the Holocaust and World War II requires, if not the response of silence predicted by some critics, at the very least a new kind of war novel. *The Heat of the Day* is certainly that, a civilian combatant's war novel full of the claustrophobic sensations accompanying the two major innovations of total war, the massacre of civilian populations in air raids and the intensification of spying in an intricate pattern of subversion.

Yet *The Heat of the Day,* even in its total response to totalitarian war, traces the disruption of the moral and intellectual fabric of life back thread

From *Southern Humanities Review* 15, no. 2 (Spring 1981). © 1981 by Auburn University.

by thread to its sources in the normal and the traditional. To convey an experience harrowing and bizarre but immeasurably distant from that of occupied Europe and *l'univers concentrationnaire,* Bowen has devised a form capable of enclosing grotesque aberration within an ordinary realistic narrative. In fact, what may be most remarkable about this rather understated novel is its ability to express by largely traditional means some of the bleakest realities conceivable. In this novel, the fictional experiment takes place inside the artifact, not on the surface.

Bowen's earlier novels show a sensibility informed by the experiences of World War I and the Troubles in Ireland. Europe is explicitly ominous, particularly in *The House in Paris*. The nightmare foreseen there is the kind that history unfolded. The dangers of the stress between surface propriety and repressed viciousness are analyzed expertly in *The Death of the Heart*. The private disease or dilemma has always its public dimension, and in Bowen's work the two are linked without artifice, simply by seeing into them, a process that yields new mysteries at each stage.

In *The Heat of the Day,* Bowen's concentration on the moral mysteries is at its most intense. The innocents of her earlier novels are always in quest of knowledge and faced with obstacles in that quest, but here a deeper doubt arises. Not only knowledge but the ground of knowledge is in doubt. In retrospect, as it happens, similar questions can be read in the earlier work, but now the cold queries of epistemology hurl themselves directly on the stuff of the novel: character, plot, everything down to the least detail of furnishing, phrases, and allusions. The war that is the setting and, in a deeper sense, the subject of the novel will have taken from its survivors abilities they can never regain. There is a change in the nature of uncertainty, not just the degree. Therefore the texture of existence and its rendering in the novel must be permeated by doubtfulness, ambiguity, mistake, falsity. A conviction is established, however, by the end of the novel, that the unreliability of knowledge and of people has been revealed rather than created by war, that the difficulties of knowing are inherent in the nature of human personality, in the social context, and finally in the nature of reality itself.

The literary forebear of this novel is *Hamlet*. All the puzzles and hauntings of that tragedy are still possible, but heroism is not. Qualities less grandiose will come to seem heroic enough in the bombscape of desolated possibilities. Nevertheless, echoes of *Hamlet* throughout will evoke both parallels and poignant differences.

This philosophical novel is also Pirandellian in the thoroughness of its skepticism, or almost so. The bleakness of the view, the refusal to hope for some firm ground underfoot, is incomplete. The case should not be put more positively than that, yet an English, an Anglo-Irish stubbornness in it resists the final surrender to the evasiveness of truth, and ends instead with the clearly implied possibility of a hope, or at least of a plodding common-sensical commitment to muddle on with until the missing theoretical structure can be supplied. Provisional yet not improvised, old platitude and fresh response to genocidal war, the hope lies in preservation and generation, specifically in the child nurtured with natural feeling, not cramped in a cage of orthodoxies or ideologies. Heroism without weapons, the heroism of a mother giving birth, of a child laboring to grow up, is sketched without sentimentality or bombast in the frame surrounding the main plot.

In the carefully detailed opening scene, England is evoked semi-cere-moniously. It is England and not-England, as most things to follow will be themselves and yet not. The scene is pastoral, yet not, an open-air concert in Regent's Park. The season is late, the day is ending, the audience consists of foreigners and English, including Harrison, who will act as catalyst in the plot, and Louie, who will serve as foil to the protagonist. For the foreigners, night and winter have already come. The presence of occupied Europe is first felt here. The "roofless theatre" prefigures the bombed buildings that are the most emphatic part of the setting, and the amphitheatre evokes Greek tragedy. The blood and horror of these two allusions are set against the gentility of the Viennese orchestra, remnant of international harmony and of a society now seen to have been poisoned from within, a sick rose. The incongruities of war where there should be peace, at home and in bed, begin here as Harrison goes from the concert to Stella's flat to storm the Englishman's castle from within.

In the final scene, a rite of survival, Louie completes the frame of the novel, again at six o'clock on a September evening, again under the open sky, when she walks her baby, child of some unknown soldier, up and down the path that once led to her parents' demolished house. Overhead go three bombers, then three swans, new metaphors and old in the same sky. (This celebratory aspect of the novel recalls other English novels of the same time, notably Waugh's *Brideshead Revisited* and Henry Green's *Caught* and, above all, Virginia Woolf's *Between the Acts,* which finds in the outdoor pageant the most reverberant formula for the vitality of English life under threat.)

In the main plot the ethical and epistemological questions are pinned to the page with as spare a device as any detective story. The protagonist, Stella Rodney, is confronted by the unknown Harrison, who threatens to report her lover, Robert Kelway, as a German spy, and who offers, if she will break off with Kelway and accept him instead as her lover, to hold up "quite a bit of stuff on him that I haven't turned in yet." Stella and Robert had met two years earlier, after he returned wounded from Dunkirk, and had fallen in love in the dislocated atmosphere of London under the Blitz, a setting of shattered glass and broken connections of all kinds. Stella (like her author) is the same age as the century. Her life has been danced to what Louis Aragon called "The Waltz of Twenty Years" in his poem for those old enough to fight in the first World War and still young enough for combat in the second. Stella's two brothers had been killed in the Great War. She had married a man who returned wounded, soon left her, and died soon after their divorce. The circle is completed once by their son Roderick, now a soldier, and again by Robert, another war-wounded man.

The story, crossed by two subplots that give it depth and definition, traces Stella's efforts to decide the truth of the accusation of treason and to see what she will find herself able to do about that truth when and if it can be known. If war is a territory, Robert has been for Stella "a habitat" within it, out of focus partly because he is too close to her. Her moral and tactical dilemmas are fused. Every conceivable move is blocked by the terms of secrecy and conspiracy. Indecision, denial, the hunt for evidence, and ill-timed half-formed decisions consume time. As with Hamlet, it is never possible precisely to distinguish her necessary tactical delays from the strategies of moral reluctance. Either can masquerade as the other. Confronted finally with the accusation, Robert at first denies but later admits its truth. Then, knowing himself watched and perhaps trapped, he climbs to the roof of Stella's building and either falls or leaps to his death in the street where agents may or may not have been waiting to capture him.

The element of melodrama in this plot is transmuted in the text by a controlled style and by the placing of emphasis. As in the novels of Woolf and Forster, the "big" events of violence or spectacular action are skirted or subordinated, in a clear enough comment on the popular belief that the drama is there in the body sprawled on the street or the bodies connecting in bed. Even the inner drama makes little enough of the personal outcome, dwarfed as it is by the gruesome tragedies numbered in millions. The book follows the progress of the war from the tides of Dunkirk to the tides of the invasion, with clear intent to emphasize the public dimension of private life as well as the usually underestimated connection between our individual experiences and their political and philosophical bases.

If this aspect suggests the history plays as well as *Hamlet*, that is appropriate, so much does the book resound with the idea of England. Still *Hamlet,* quintessential drama of doubt, ambiguity, and guilt, remains the point of reference throughout. The echoes are ubiquitous though seldom obvious. Guilt is announced by a questionable voice but is difficult to prove. Love is tainted by the idea of this guilt. Family bonds are askew. Mothers are unchaste. Intrigue twines every move. There is feigned and real madness, a funeral, a voyage, a pair of grave clowns, a son with an array of fathers, a possible but not proven suicide, sounds of distant battle, inheritance interrupted, two female avatars of Polonius, a scholar-soldier taken from the university to assume the burdens of his country and his family, references to flowers and to theatre, a subplot that is an extended pun on dumb show, and at the end a most humble Fortinbras, a working-class bastard wheeled on in a perambulator.

Echoes may be brief, as in: "Hired cars of this type could some pretty curious tales unfold, I shouldn't wonder," or extended travesties:

> Blow your nose, though, because how you ought to look at it is this way—being elderly your dad was bound to have gone soon in the course of nature; you can't say death's so unnatural; it's just the manner. Also you've got to think how your Mum and Dad were united at the last, haven't you, and. . . .

The two clown-figures are women, as are the two Polonius-speakers, and the Hamlet-figure is Stella, a woman not a hero but as near one as time and circumstance permit. Like other characters in this novel, she is neither flat nor round but translucent. Whatever is needed for her role in the action is given, but not with the richness of individual life that flourishes where a character has room to act and a continuous world to act upon. Stella lacks opacity in part because of her very naturalness. Such a character is seldom met in fiction: an intelligent, attractive woman about forty, ladylike and thoughtful, not a prude, not a snob. No special emphasis is given to the unexceptional facts of her life: that she does important work, has raised a son who turned out well, lives alone, has a stable love affair without tears or pretense, always has whiskey in the house but may not have cake. She and her son like and respect each other. All this the novel takes for granted, but such women are as rare in fiction as they are familiar in life.

Now Stella, having to face the unknowable and face it alone (the shadow of Beckett not out of place), goes through a painful initiation, a death more final than "the death of the heart." Innocence destroyed by experience has been called Bowen's characteristic theme, and that theme has a changed relevance here. Stella, far from an innocent in the usual sense, now loses, along with her whole society, which is older and more experienced than she, a kind of innocence that can never be regained. Bowen's most dogmatic and best known statement on the subject is: "No, it is not only our fate but our business to lose innocence, and once we have lost that it is futile to attempt a picnic in Eden." The idea that innocence is pernicious is pure Shaw, and Bowen subscribes also to the Shavian corollary that the illusions of any society are profoundly dangerous. Stella belongs to a society that has long lived as though certain verities were eternal, or at least as though there *were* verities. The world before the war now comes to seem like the world before the Fall. But a glance back at Bowen's earlier work shows that a serpent had already visited in various guises. The settled world in which her children study to survive is not really settled, and hardly anyone in it has grown up. But in the absence of extreme situations the surface holds or soon scabs over. To register the shock of war, a character who has passed through those earlier shocks of initiation is needed.

Stella, a star by whom two lost men try to find their way, has her years, intelligence, social connections, standards, and a clear sense of her own identity. She is fairly autonomous. Love is far from being her whole existence. Like Hamlet, she will not be content with rash action for its own sake. She wants to do the right things for the right reasons. Yet her part in the action, though central, is passive, laid upon her by outside forces. The terms of her dilemma hold her almost paralyzed in her struggle.

This constraint is representative of women's lives in war and even in peace. As one character points out, men make the decisions. The novel reminds us that women are never safe from the consequences. Little has been said in prose or poetry about women and war in modern times. As Sheila Rowbotham says in *Hidden from History* of World War I, "The problems of the men in readjusting to civilian life was a common theme of the literature of the post-war era. But the pyschological experience of the women found very little serious expression." The same might be said, with modifications, of World War II. Stella Rodney is emblematic, a woman bereft of brothers and husband, her only child awaiting orders to go into battle, her household dismantled, the temporary roof over her head threatened by air raids, and the war of betrayals now moving right into her bed.

It is not surprising that Stella should have been chosen by Vida E. Markovič as one of nine exemplary characters for analysis in *The Changing Face: Disintegration of Personality in the Twentieth Century British Novel, 1900–1950*. Stella represents for her the generation disabled by war and its aftermath, a generation characterized by an inability to act, a tendency to acquiescence born of a desire to feel as little as possible. Yet Markovič also sees in her "the stubborn persistence of heroic virtue." Having herself lived in occupied Belgrade, Markovič is sharply aware of the "tragic hour in which ordinary people . . . are suddenly faced with only two alternatives: heroism or treachery." Although Stella's alternatives do not involve torture and death, she does share that fear for one's ability to survive morally that Markovič considers worse than the fear of death. The dangers may be less hideous, but the choices are less clear. Which course *is* heroism, which treachery? Or is it in fact a choice between one treachery and another, a choice that modulates the idea of heroism into a minor key?

E. M. Forster's poignant hope that, if forced to choose between betraying his country and betraying his friend, he would betray his country, becomes doubly poignant when the country that made such moral elegance possible itself stands in danger of destruction. The Forster view, as much a luxury of British ascendancy as tea or silk or spices, becomes another casualty of this war. Nor will there ever be a way for Stella to know after the fact whether she has done right. This is darkness without hope of even a retrospective light. Shaw gives his Don Juan the aphorism that applies here: "[T]o be in hell is to drift: to be in heaven is to steer." For Stella, as for Hamlet, hell consists in being left with nothing sure to steer by.

The last word about Stella must be more equivocal. The author, introducing her, sums up this way: "Generous and spirited, to a fault not unfeeling, she was not wholly admirable; but who is?" For this quite admirable character is in some sense akin to the treasonous Robert: "There existed between them the complicity of brother and sister twins, counterpart flowering of a temperament identical at least with regard to love."

Robert Kelway, known only from the viewpoint of Stella, does not appear until after the accusation against him has been made, so that he is seen from the first in the light of doubt. His motivation for acting as a German spy, which has given the critics great trouble, depends heavily on defects of personality traced back to his home life. The evacuation from Dunkirk, which he regards as a failure of the British military rather than a triumph of the British civilian, has evidently wounded him in spirit as well as in body. Perhaps, like his father before him, he has become "impotent in all ways but one."

Robert's evasiveness at the first tentative mention of Harrison—he changes the subject, significantly, first to neckties, then to bed—is our first glimpse of his deviousness, a style rooted in his home life, which is exposed when Stella goes with him to meet his mother and sister at Holme Dene. He tries to evade this visit also, mocking her: "—research? My case history?" Holme Dene is in fact a textbook case, contorted, compulsive, false, lightless, inhuman, although on the surface utterly proper, overbearingly so. The house is announced by its sign: "CAUTION: CONCEALED DRIVE." Holme Dene really is a den, also a labyrinth and a spiderweb. Without Gothic trappings, the house is the most sinister in Bowen's work, in which places are so meaningful. The name surely derives from Dene-hole, a mysterious type of archaeological find, a shaft sunk in a chalk formation, widening out underground, thought to have been used as a hiding place in time of war. Primeval rat-like mental processes are also characteristic of the Kelways. The psychoanalytical overtones are not obscure.

> A backdrop of trees threw into relief a tennis pavilion, a pergola, a sundial, a rock garden, a dovecote, some gnomes, a seesaw, a grouping of rusticated seats, and a bird-bath.

(We are obviously in the presence of what, in Jane Austen, would be termed "improvements." By contrast, the Irish estate will be seen to be "unimproved.")

The lounge is "blackly furnished with antique oak, papered art brown and curtained with copper chenille." And so on. The decor is twisting, cryptic, theatric. This house, although always vaguely up for sale, has been permeated by the spirit of Mrs. Kelway.

> By sometimes looking, by sometimes even not looking, across the furnished lawn, she projected Holme Dene: this was a bewitched wood. If her power came to an end at the white gate, so did the world.

The child's world certainly would.

The motionless Kelway mother and her frenetic daughter share a psychic disease one symptom of which is the essential rudeness of those who cannot honor or even recognize the humanity of other people. They focus instead on mechanical details. Introduced, Mrs. Kelway goes right on to, "But what became of the taxi?" She says not *who* but, "What do you mean by Roderick?" Her obsessive management of three pennies that may be needed for extra postage on a package addressed three times stands on the shoulders of myth to announce her compulsive busyness covering a sickening void. Mother and daughter are standard family fascists in their treatment of the little niece and nephew who live with them, suspecting, squelching, chilling. Everything is super-supervised, triply accounted for, and cloacally contained. In this prim repressiveness and in their smug invasions of the children's privacy it is easy to see the process that prevented Robert from developing any belief in himself or his country. In the case of nonfalsifiable manias, the only alternative to submission may seem to be a complete smash, which is just what Robert hopes for from the defeat of England. The house is in effect a private madhouse, mother and daughter each doubling as keeper and inmate. If this, with a mother called Muttikins and a gnome-infested lawn, is not enough to account for Robert, what would be too much?

Like the gnomes on the lawn, the Kelway women are both rootless and immobile. The impermanence of the house is Bowen's comment on a social phenomenon.

> Everything can be shifted, lock, stock, and barrel. After all, everything was brought here from someone [*sic*] else, with the intention of being moved again—like touring scenery from theatre to theatre. Reassemble it anywhere; you get the same illusion.

Pretentious in size and in its fake antiquity, the house is typical of a state of mind, a danger:

> The English, she could only tell herself, were extraordinary—for if this were not England she did not know what it was. You could not account for this family headed by Mrs. Kelway simply by saying that it was middle-class, because that left you asking, middle of what? She saw the Kelways suspended in the middle of nothing.

Here somewhere in the proper, conventional home life that denies impulse and lacks all delight is the etiology of treason, and if not as simple and obvious as some other, probably more accurate for that reason.

In retrospect, it seems strange that so many reviewers of *The Heat of the Day,* writing soon after the end of the war, when stories like his were fresh in memory, should have found Robert's pro-German activities so improbable. In 1949 when the book was published, many intellectuals had just returned from serving in military intelligence where they must have encountered more than one agent of Robert's type. To have made him pro-Soviet, though easier to motivate, would for that very reason have eased the moral dilemma and vitiated the mystery and horror. Of course he does not smell like a spy, but his plausibility is more than plausible: it is one expression of the root paradox of the book. An agent who had Suspicious Character written all over him would not have been trusted with official secrets. One of the givens of the novel is this mirroring effect that inevitably reverses the truth it reports. The craft of the novelist appears here also in leaving spaces blank that would remain blank in the character's experience, instead of supplying a tidy motivation. If the Eichmann trial fails to explain Eichmann, the novelist had better not neatly explain her minor pro-Nazi, who is not even for the Nazis so much as he is for the smash that he imagines will wipe the slate clean for England. His revulsion has much in common with Birkin's "hare sitting up" harangue in *Women in Love*, a nausea at English society as it is. To explain a negativism so general would be intrusive and false. Roderick's comment on army secrecy may apply here: "In fact . . . it comes to seem fishy when one *is* told anything."

If Robert were revised or explained, the enigmatic mode of the novel would be as badly served as its historical truth. Even the word "treason" is too definite in this equivocal context. It belongs to an antecedent world in which loyalty to one's homeland could be treated in epic certainty as a good. That universe of traditional song and story lasted until the war in which Stella's brothers died, then cracked forever. Robert speaks bitterly of these dead as "lucky to die before the illusion had broken down" and of their war as "a troubadour's war." His only heritage from his defeated father and the insane certitudes of his mother is doubt—of himself, of his country, of meaning. It is also possible to become a hero resisting the state instead of fighting for it, but that kind of certainty must come from within, where Robert has no firm center to consult. In this he is one of many: the outwardly presentable *collaborateurs* filmed by Ophüls for *The Sorrow and the Pity*, the English writers who flirted with fascism in the twenties, the long list of dangerous men with ordinary faces. There is a natural reluctance to cry, "mon semblable, mon frère," but this novel is stern in its insistence on the insecurity of moral boundaries and the volatility of the self in exploded contexts.

If it seems implausible next that Stella should have remained so unsuspecting through two years of intimacy, it matters that they have met and loved each other in a social vacuum, with future, past, family, friends, jaggedly broken away from them. They have lived in the present because the territory of war contains no other time. The moment of their declaration of love is interrupted by a bomb falling nearby:

> It was the demolition of an entire moment: he and she had stood at attention till the glissade stopped. What they *had* been both saying, neither of them ever now were to know. Most first words have the nature of being trifling; theirs from having been lost began to have the significance of a lost clue.

The loss of language and the hunt for clues begin for them that early.

The fine discriminations of the novel make its patterns of doubling and darkness more than a literary flourish. The congruence between Stella and Robert, for example, is only partial. When Robert finally talks about his reasons, he says, "Look at your free people—mice let loose in the middle of the Sahara. It's insupportable—what is it but a vacuum?" Earlier Stella at Mount Morris had thought: "For her part, she would never agree that Roderick had been victimized: he had been fitted into a destiny: better, it seemed to her, than freedom in nothing." As mere statements these two are parallel, but in practice radically opposed. One is an apology for tyranny, the other a claim for the values of responsibility. Only equivocation could reconcile the two. As with her sense of time, which some characters in the novel have, the others remaining totally dependent on clocks, Stella has a sense of what abstractions mean in moral or human terms.

Here Bowen's perceptions in the novelist's great arena, the place where social, psychological, and moral issues fuse, show their great strength. Stella and Robert might agree in conversation that "freedom in nothing" is not the greatest good, but Stella's idea springs from different sources, refers to different specifics, and results in opposite loyalties and actions.

These affinities and differences are set off by the third character in the triangle. Harrison, this third, is a stranger with only one bit of name, no antecedents or credentials. Nothing is known about his life or family except that he once says, "I have never been loved." If the others are translucent, he is transparent, almost featureless, a figure as dangerous as a piece of exposed machinery and as unconscious of malice. He is the carrier of the dilemma merely, himself neither evil nor powerful. As Mother Courage says of the rampaging soldiery, "Thank God they're human. You can bribe them." You can make a deal with Harrison. He is willing.

It turns out that there are two Roberts in the novel, agent and double-agent being doubles, although Harrison does not reveal that his name also is Robert until the other is dead. There are subtler clues to their affinity, quite apart from the strange notion that one might simply replace the other in Stella's life. Both are physically asymmetrical, Robert's legs uneven from his war wound, Harrison's eyes seeming to be at different heights. One has no home, the other a home that is a furnished vacuum. William Heath comments acutely: "The fact that they cannot be finally distinguished, even by name, is Miss Bowen's bitterest comment on the moral chaos she explores."

Harrison can hardly recognize the concept of home:

"Where exactly do you live? I have no idea."
"There are always two or three places where I can turn in."
"But for instance, where do you keep your razor?"
"I have two or three razors," he said in an absent tone.

Considering how potent the idea of house and home is in Bowen's fiction and how much is made in this novel of the bombing of homes and uprooting of families, Harrison's lack of any homing instinct says much about his lack of identity. His crookedness, apparent in word and deed, is signified also by his uneven eyes, which figure in the mosaic of light and sight images. Long before an American president was to announce to his country, "I am not a crook," Harrison gives his own slant on wartime: "[F]or me the principal thing is that it's a time when I'm not a crook." Of course in wartime, although with his distorted vision he cannot see it, he still operates like a crook, but temporarily and unreliably in a better cause.

In the book's sampler of spoiled language, Harrison's is a characteristically disjointed uneasy mixture of the cheap and the stilted. At the funeral where he first meets Stella he is full of phrases like: "at a show like this . . . I having, as one might say, so oft heard your praises sung. . . . one puts two and two together. . . . a stiff . . ." His social shoddiness is matched by his intellectual and emotional shoddiness. We are told of "a crisis . . . of his emotional idiocy . . . as unnerving as might be a brainstorm in someone without a brain." The effect is heightened by portraying Harrison almost entirely in dialogue.

Of course he does have a brain, a mechanical brain good at tactics, and he is drawn to Stella by a specific attraction to identity, integrity, by a wish to enter "the first idea he had of poetry—her life." Frog and princess, they meet only because the war has tossed a ball down a well.

This psychological lack reflects back on Robert, his double. The two are opponents at a chess board, seeing their moves as maneuvers rather than real battles, because principle would have to be grounded in self, and neither has any assured self. Though prepared to destroy Robert, Harrison says, "I haven't a thing against him." Returning to her flat in the company of Harrison seems to Stella "a grotesque series of variations" on her returns with Robert. The idea is nailed too explicitly at the end when Stella thinks "it was Robert who had been the Harrison," but for the most part more subtly, as in the Irish steward's conflation of the two names as Robertson.

The pairing gives credibility to the idea of Robert as one of a dangerous class, the detached detachable souls with careers in power and conspiracy. Authoritarian societies build on their petty tyrannies and unaccountability. More than one metaphor hints at this potential in the "loyal" Harrison and implies that fascism depends as much on lack of principle as on any doctrine. Stella says he rings up "like the Gestapo," and he looks around her drawing room "like a German in Paris." Lacking a self, he can be neither pro- nor anti- either Nazis or England. He moves counters around in a contest without content. When Stella speaks of duty to her country, he understands that idea only as another piece to be brought into play and merely considers what it is worth to his game. The final measure of his crook's patriotism is his willingness to dicker about letting Robert go on spying for the Germans. Attempts to place Harrison on the side of right completely miss this. Doubling works both ways.

Set against this weightlessness and nullity, a connection between self and soil, self and history, is built into other elements of the novel. In a significant phrase, the narrator says that Stella "had it in her to have been an honest woman." Without being heroic, certain characters have something "in them." Those who have something "in them" also have connections with something outside themselves, something older. What that something may be is not entirely amenable to statement but can be inferred from the two subplots, one extending vertically through family history (and the hope of continuation), the other horizontally across social classes, to sketch a fictional graph of England, the flawed treasure, civilization.

Continuity and tradition enter the disjointed present along the axes of these subplots. The death of a cousin makes Stella's son heir to an estate in Ireland. Cousin Francis has died without issue, his wife, Cousin Nettie, a witty gloss on the mad-wife figure in the Gothic novel, having long since removed to a home for the harmlessly deranged.

Roderick might pun as Hamlet does on being too much in the sun. He has a dead father, a kind of step-father in Robert, and now becomes a cousin's heir. Roderick was conceived during his parents' honeymoon at the house he now inherits. House and estate are a heavy responsibility that Roderick must shoulder as he does his heavy pack. The thread between the two burdens is lightly drawn, in, for example, references to a mousetrap, which tie both lightly also to *Hamlet*. The importance of this ancestral home in neutral Ireland is emphasized in the structure of the novel. The chapter in which Stella visits there to settle arrangements for her son, because he is under age and under orders, stands exactly at the center of the book. The turning points of the military and psychological action coincide. There the news of Montgomery's victory at El Alamein reaches Stella. There she decides to confront Robert directly, like Hamlet, returning from a sea voyage ready for action.

The symmetry of the structure goes further. In the first half of the book Stella travels to Wisteria Lodge for the funeral of Cousin Francis and visits Holme Dene with Robert. In the second half, Roderick visits Cousin Nettie at Wisteria Lodge and Robert visits his mother and sister at Holme Dene. Mount Morris is, however, a far from simple keystone.

Coming to Mount Morris out of the territory of war puts Stella in touch with a standard of normality and a pastoral calm, but even this setting

is profoundly marked by ambiguity. The house is in almost erotic touch
with the natural scene, woods and river and fields:

> This valley cleavage into the distance seemed like an offering to
> the front windows; in return the house devoted the whole muted
> fervour of its being to a long gaze.

In its association with family ties, responsibility, and victory, Mount Morris
is clearly a good thing, a bond with the past but also the future. Here Stella
speculates on her son's future wife and the changes she may make in the
house. The unremitting effort that goes into maintaining a house is set, by
implication, against the moment it takes for a bomb to destroy everything.

Yet the contrast is far from simple. Binding past and present through
the imagery of light and sight, total war penetrates here in a surprising
shortage of candles and lamp oil, but the darkness of a familiar house is
lightened by other senses. Older wars also haunt the place. Bowen is always
conscious that the Anglo-Irish "got their position and drew their power
from a situation that shows an inherent wrong." The meaning of this house
is further modified by the existence of another across the sea in England, the
kind of house that is called a "home" because it is not one. Cousin Nettie
had fled there (to save her insanity?) from her cousin-husband. Lucid, even
acute, although with inspired flights from lucidity, this aged Ophelia in her
flowery setting poses one of the characteristic riddles of the novel. Roderick
ponders the catch in her voluntary confinement:

> There had not been a touch of hysteria about this: on the con-
> trary, it had been policy—Hamlet had got away with it; why
> should not she? But there had been doubts about Hamlet. . . .
> could anyone who voluntarily espoused Wisteria Lodge be *quite*
> normal?—but then again, normal: what was that?

Named for a plant with lush flowers and strangling stems, the Lodge reflects
back on the other constricted, respectable, surface-saving house, Holme
Dene: "This powerhouse of nothingness, hive of lives in abeyance, seemed
to Roderick no more peculiar than any other abode." Perhaps even the
family home, Mount Morris.

Something incestuous lurks in Cousin Nettie's trouble. She wears half-
mourning for her late husband. "Mourning for a cousin—he was my cousin, you know. There should never have been any other story." The cousin-
husband recalls Hamlet's uncle-father and aunt-mother. Ancestral houses
may have their value, but Nettie says, "There have been too many ances-

tors. . . . We are so mixed up by this time that it's a wonder we are anything at all."

This portrait recognizes that madness may mean seeing more, not less. Cousin Nettie has "the eyes of an often-rebuked clairvoyante." Only she can tell Roderick the truth about his parents' divorce, confided in her by his father just because she *was* so odd. One thing she sees is that men make the decisions but men do not "notice" things, and that allows them to keep going. She projects the realization that women are powerless, in jeopardy, and aware. Stella intuits this truth when she sees herself in the old looking glass and muses on what their traditional role costs women.

> After all, was it not chiefly here in this room and under this illusion that Cousin Nettie Morris—and who now knew how many more before her?—had been pressed back, hour by hour, by the hours themselves, into cloudland? Ladies had gone not quite mad . . . from in vain listening for meaning in the loudening tick of the clock . . . her kind knew no choices, made no decisions. . . . No, knowledge was not to be kept from them, reached them by intimations. . . . So, there had been cases of the enactment of ignorance having become too much, insupportable inside those sheltered heads. . . . Their conversation was a twinkling surface over their deep silence. Virtually, they were never to speak at all.

Feigned and real madness, feigned and real sanity, a growing conviction that most of the behavior people pigeonhole so casually is really a compound of elements themselves compounds, all these considerations heap up comment on that quintessence of dust out of which such complicated flowers grow. For all its function as a standard of normality, the ancestral home is not sentimentalized, the past not glorified.

The other subplot suggests the continuity of English life across class barriers. In her preface to *The Demon Lover*, a collection of her wartime short stories, Bowen says, "In war this feeling of slight differentiation was suspended: I felt one with, and just like, everybody else." In this wartime novel, Bowen creates, in the character of Louie Lewis, an incongruous but recognizable variation on Stella. Poles apart in appearance, education, class, manners, and almost everything else, the two share essentials both in their fate as women and war victims, and in the soundness of their responses, a kind of ethical common sense that they share just as the two Roberts share a lack of it. Louie Lewis, a factory worker whose parents have been killed in an air raid and whose husband has gone off to war, is an audacious literary experiment, a portrait of an inarticulate, semiliterate, premoral woman whose epic heroism goes beyond endurance to stubborn self-determination. She and her friend Connie are the equivalent of Shakespeare's clowns, one vital, one mechanical, whose attempts to seize the tragic theme lend it poignance through travesty. They parody the glib formulas of the educated classes, judge and misjudge their betters accordingly, throwing an abashing light on the rhetoric above them.

As her name hints, Louie Lewis defies categories, including those of gender. There is nothing feminine about her, although she is quite female biologically. Living residue of her dead mother and father, she will also be both mother and father to her child, as Stella has been to hers. Her doubled name seems to signify that her family will be compressed for this generation in her sturdy body and weak intellect as in the neck of an hourglass. Like Roderick Rodney, she carries the double burden because the time is out of joint.

Her rapprochement with Stella takes place with symbolic emphasis at their one meeting during a crucial encounter between Stella and Harrison. Joined in opposition to him and in some natural affinity, these two incongruous sisters join hands at one remove when Stella picks up Louie's glove from the floor with a simplicity that has tacit religious overtones. Louie emits a ration of cant from her newspaper reading: "Still, as it says, we women are all in the same boat," which is false as printed and quoted, but true in some dimension beyond platitude. They go off to guide each other home, equalized in ignorance and incompetence by the blackout, wise and foolish non-virgins, both without light now.

Neither has lived by the sexual rules man-made for women. The book is dotted with dreadful or deranged women who have. A statement about Stella applies to both: "She had it in her to have been an honest woman and borne more children; she had been capable of more virtue than the succeeding years had left her able to show." Both women are capable of sadness, a human quality to be prized by contrast with the metallic characters around them. The affinity is strong enough that words, usually the hardest thing for Louie to find, come to her hypnotically: "A soul astray," she later says of Stella. Although Louie's movements are tangential to those of the main characters, her relation to the theme is finally concentric.

Netted in the fabric of ambiguities and deceptions, the main plot of treason and detection shares three arrays of imagery with the two subplots, one of Mount Morris, landed gentry, the other of Louie Lewis, working-class woman. One set of images relates to houses and the scarred spaces where houses once stood, a second to light, sight, eyes and windows, pictures, mirrors, a third to the breakdown of language and communication.

Houses, which in Bowen's work have a life of their own that goes beyond setting, atmosphere, or even symbol, have been described along with the characters who belong to them, necessarily, as the relationship is symbiotic. They range from Holme Dene, which is overdetermined, to Stella's flat, which expresses only the taste of some previous tenants. The two houses shown capable of nurturing life are, paradoxically, Mount Morris, which produced no heirs of its own, and the totally demolished house in which Louie's parents died.

The obscurity of the truth has its metaphor ready-made in the wartime blackout, which is reinforced by pervasive images, seldom obtrusive, of optical illusion and the ambiguity of pictures. Often in *The Heat of the Day* one may see what is not there, fail to see what is, or see clearly something that is not what it seems. There is darkness or too much light. Two climactic scenes take place in painful glare, the meeting of Stella and Robert, at which they fall in love in "a dazzling blend of sun and electric light," and the meeting at which Stella rejects Harrison finally in the hallucinatory cafe: "The phenomenon was the lighting, more powerful even than could be accounted for by the bald white globes screwed aching to the low white ceiling." Robert's admission of his guilt comes in an even more explicitly hellish light: "Her room was bathed in a red appearance of heat from the electric fire . . . this red half-dark of so many nights having within the moment become infernal." Most scenes, however, are darkened by night and blackout curtains. Only in Ireland is there a tolerable mixture of light and shade. Sun is shining through the leaves when Stella hears of Montgomery's breakthrough at El Alamein. (All she can hear at first is another Shakespearean echo of lovers crossed by war, "Egypt!") At Mount Morris, she knows the house well enough to find her way even in the dark.

Indoors, where most scenes except those in Ireland and the framing scenes at beginning and end take place, the characters confront each other among glassy versions of reality. Stella observes Harrison's first entrance in a mirror, facing photographs, on the mantle, of her son and her lover. In the mirror at Mount Morris she sees herself "for the moment immortal as a portrait. . . . She wore the look of everything she had lost the secret of being." Actual portraits cast Pirandellian doubts on reality itself. His childhood snapshots raise the question, "And was, indeed, Robert himself fictitious?" Louie takes no comfort from the photograph of her absent husband, which she sees because she dusts it daily, but does not look at. Cousin

Nettie's mind is revealed in a picture of the Titanic going down with lights ablaze, in macabre scenes that are permitted in her room because their "neutralizing prettiness" belies their real content, but no pictures of Mount Morris: "They are so dark-looking. And why should I want a picture of anything I have seen?" At Holme Dene even a natural sunset yields "a chemically yellowing light" and Robert looks "like a young man in Technicolour." Finally Robert escapes from capture and from life through a skylight that has been trapdoored over, a compound image of his pyschic life.

Eyes are as ambiguous as light. Harrison, with his odd eyes, claims to know Robert "by sight." The devious Kelway family defines truthfulness: "Our father always used to look us straight in the eye." As a result, Robert says, "The jelly of an eye, not to speak of whatever else there may be in it, has been unseemly to me ever since." That jelly, with its echo of *King Lear*, is a perverse way of viewing eyes.

As sight can deceive, so can language, the other source of knowledge that is subject to sophistication. In both dialogue and narrative, words carry secondary meanings that raise doubt and reveal morbid or equivocal thoughts suppressed in the speaker's mind. The contorted syntax characteristic of Bowen's style is here an exact vehicle for the expression of awkward speech or twisted thought. Apart from deliberate deceptions, conversations unintentionally misfire throughout the novel, often as a result of Harrison's underworld taciturnity.

> "Ever mentioned my name?"
> "You mean, has he mentioned your name to me?"
> "No; have you mentioned my name to him?"

But Stella herself, engaged in war work, is capable of "commanding a sort of language in which nothing need be ever exactly said." Even the will leaving Mount Morris to Roderick contains an ambiguous modifier: house and land are left to him "in the hope that he may care in his own way to carry on the old tradition." Stella wonders whether the caring or the carrying on is to be done in his own way.

Misuse apart, language is itself a questionable commodity. Stella asks Robert:

> "Only, why are you against this country?"
> "Country?"
> "This, where we are."
> "I don't see what you mean—what *do* you mean? Country?— there are no more countries left; nothing but names."

Robert explains himself here even better than he means to—the appropriate reverse of the conversations in which characters fail to convey what they mean. His alienation shows in his way of parting words from their referents. He could say in bitter truth what Hamlet, in response to, "What do you read, my lord?" says only mockingly: "Words, words, words." In his final confrontation with Stella he says:

> "What is repulsing you is the idea of 'betrayal' I suppose, isn't it? In you the hangover from the word? Don't you understand that all that language is dead currency? How they keep on playing shop with it all the same: even you do. Words, words."

Hamlet's satiric dissociation of words from matter becomes here the actual madness of assuming that because "betrayal" is a word, it is *only* a word. Reductivism (the eye as a vile jelly) is characteristic of authoritarian minds like Robert's, minds seeking more control than is humanly possible. The commercial imagery recalls Polonius, another character in whom sentence crowds out nature.

For Stella and her son words have not come apart from the meanings. Roderick finds a word real enough to shy at: "But why should they arrest him as a—as what you said?" Louie, conscious of her own lack of words as a handicap and an almost physical agony, admires Stella from a distance for her ability to speak "beautifully." But this we know has been damaged. Stella has found her conversation with Robert a burlesque of itself and "no other vocabulary, least of all that of silence, at once offered itself." In response, Robert speaks "as a man who . . . casts round him for words at random, realises their futility before uttering them, but does all the same utter them, as the only means of casting them from him again, rejected."

The calculated corruption of language by fascist regimes is implied, as well as the reciprocal effect Orwell pointed out in "Politics and the English Language." That may be why Louie, who can scarcely read or speak, is sounder than most, climbing under instead of over the barriers.

Believing, perhaps naïvely, that words still matter, Roderick also believes meaning should be possible. And meaning brings Shakespeare to his mind. He worries about his mother, left to live on with unanswerable questions:

> "I couldn't bear to think of you waiting on and on and on for something, something that in a flash would give what Robert did . . . enormous meaning like there is in a play of Shakespeare's. . . . You want me to be posterity? But then, Robert's

> dying of what he did will not always be there, won't last like a
> book or picture. . . . Because, I suppose art is the only thing that
> can go on mattering once it has stopped hurting?"

The subsidiary motif of time works in a similar way. The war puts time
literally out of joint. Daylight lasts two hours longer, but nights are chthonic
in shelters and blackout. In Ireland, time is slowed, almost to a standstill.
Like language, time is diagnostic of character. The mechanical men and
women who live by clocks and timetables are the same ones who have no
moral horizon left when the world turns upside down. Stella and her son,
Louie and perhaps her infant son, who is in gestation through nine months
of the book's year, possess a vital sense that keeps them level with time,
politics, and other people. The fact that Stella's watch never quite synchro-
nizes with Robert's is one sign that the affinity between them is incomplete
and that the moral gulf is fixed even though the rest is flux.

In details like these the fabric has been so finely woven that only small
patches can be picked apart for analysis, but the effect is produced by the
whole tapestry of the novel. The broad outlines that emerge from all the
intricacy of detail show darkness and light mingled and not without meaning. In its unflinching treatment of the dire losses in certainty of our century,
losses for which the Victorian crisis of faith now seems a mere rehearsal (if
not a premonition), Elizabeth Bowen's war novel shows a vision closer to
those of Kafka, Pirandello, Camus, and Beckett than to that of Jane Austen,
the comparison of choice for critics of her work.

The essential difference between Bowen's response and those of her
contemporaries on the Continent may be implicit in the anonymous baby or
the young soldier who may live to father children in an ancient house. The
meaning of these and other ritual elements remains, like so much else in the
book, an enigma, but that is very different from a denial of meaning. Bowen
herself was among the first to give expression to the idea of a literature of
silence coming out of World War II, although distanced in the words of a
character in one of her wartime short stories:

> "Henry is probably right," said Ronald Cuffe, "in considering
> that this—this outrage is *not* important. There is no place for it
> in human experience; it apparently cannot make a place of its
> own. It will have no literature."

Yet even the unspeakable has had a literature and is beginning to have a
body of literary criticism as well. This is as it should be, an effort not just to

memorialize, but to seek meaning of some sort in experiences that themselves baffle all response.

Bowen's variations on the enigma she proposes are derived from a generation and a culture that belong still to the old order, although she is too honest a writer to treat as unfallen the Europe that produced the monster. Her style and values derive from that prewar world, but she has used the novel form for heuristic purposes, treating it always as a vehicle for both intelligence and intellect. Perhaps only a writer so civilized can offer such a faithful critique of her own civilization.

HERMIONE LEE

The Bend Back: A World of Love *(1955)*, The Little Girls *(1964)*, *and* Eva Trout *(1968)*

What fails in the air of our present-day that we cannot breathe it?

The "awful illumination" of war confirmed, on a vast scale, Elizabeth Bowen's personal vision of a denatured and dispossessed civilisation. "There's been a stop in our senses and in our faculties that's made everything around us so much dead matter." "How are we to live without natures? . . . So much flowed through people; so little flows through us . . . All we can do is imitate love or sorrow." These characteristic utterances (from "Summer Night" and "The Happy Autumn Fields") are spoken out of limbo, by people disinherited from a past rich in emotions and certainties, and prisoners to a future which requires "genius" to be lived in at all. The paradigmatic voice of her wartime writing might be that of the young soldier in her radio play of 1946 about Trollope, who dreams on a railway journey, that he is speaking to Trollope and explaining to him his love of the novels:

> "We're homesick for anything right-and-tight . . . The whole way of life that is quite, apparently, gone . . . I think your novels are a support against the sort of *hopelessness* we're inclined to feel . . . It's essential for us these days, to believe in people, and in their power to live . . . we long for what's ordinary."

Elizabeth Bowen's postwar writing deals more than ever with the failure of feeling and certainty in modern civilization, and with the need for

From *Elizabeth Bowen: An Estimation.* © 1981 by Hermione Lee. Barnes & Noble Books, 1981.

consolatory retreats into memory and fantasy. The last three novels reiterate
a distaste for contemporaneity: "Her time, called hers because she was
required to live in it and had no other, was in bad odour, and no wonder . . .
too much had been going on for too long." "Nothing's real any more . . .
There's a tremendous market for prefabricated feelings." "What becomes of
anyone's nature?" In her writing about contemporary fiction she finds "an
increasing discrepancy between facts, or circumstances, and feeling, or the
romantic will," an increasing compulsion to retreat from the nullity of
modern life into "the better days":

> Now, after a second war, with its excoriations, grinding imper-
> sonality, obliteration of so many tracks and landmarks, heart
> and imagination once more demand to be satisfied . . . Can this
> demand be met only by recourse to life in the past? It at present
> seems so. . . .
>
> . . . What fails in the air of our present-day that we cannot
> breathe it? Why cannot the confidence in living, the engagement
> with living, the prepossession with living be re-won?

Just as the war answered to Elizabeth Bowen's conception of her civilization, so the conditions of the postwar life in the West seemed to confirm her
diagnosis. The three novels she wrote in the fifties and sixties are about
displacement, alienation and the search for consolation. They "bend back"—
into her own past, in that they return to prewar Ireland and to schooldays in
Kent, and into the characters' past, in that two of the three novels describe
attempts to summon up lost time. The last novel is set in the present, but its
characters are at a loss in an alien world.

In their emphasis on dislocation, on the discrepancy between "fact, or
circumstances, and feeling, or the romantic will," the last novels confirm her
lifelong attitudes to existence. More privately, they arise from the rather
unhappy circumstances of Elizabeth Bowen's old age. *A World of Love* was
begun in Ireland after the death of Alan Cameron, and the shabbiness of its
Irish house reflects, as Victoria Glendinning suggests, her "own predicament
at Bowen's Court." After the sale and demolition of Bowen's Court she
continued to go to Ireland, most often as the guest of the Vernons at Kin-
sale, and since the early fifties she had been spending a good deal of time in
America, and in Rome (visits which resulted in a fanciful and indulgent
travel-book, *A Time in Rome*). But she had no home. Her attempts to settle
down in England took the form of journeys back into her past. She first took
a flat in Headington, in a house belonging to Isaiah Berlin, and then, in
1965, bought a house in Hythe. In her sixties she developed lung cancer.

The biography insists that Elizabeth Bowen put a brave face on her circumstances and was active, busy and sociable until the last possible moment. The last two novels, however, communicate a painful sense of uncertainty, even of disequilibrium. Evidently there were personal reasons for this, but the unsatisfactoriness of the later work also has literary grounds. Elizabeth Bowen's fiction in the 1930s and 1940s resulted from a fruitful conjunction between her historical attitudes, her literary manner and her sense of a society. After the war her attitudes to that society seemed to be confirmed, but her literary manner was losing its usefulness. The last two novels in particular express unease not merely in their subject matter but also in an uncertainty of tone. And though *A World of Love*, her only novel of the fifties, is more like the earlier books and has some attractive atmospheric qualities, it works an outworn vein. With *Friends and Relations*, it is the most mannered of her novels, and, unlike *The Death of the Heart* or *The House in Paris*, it is sentimental about youthful innocence.

After *A World of Love* she felt the need to turn herself into a different kind of novelist. I am reminded of Virginia Woolf's reaction against *The Waves*, and her attempt to find a method which would make *The Years* into an appropriate fictional document for the thirties. Elizabeth Bowen, likewise, wanted to come to terms with the sixties. There's an illuminating reference in the biography to the influence of Iris Murdoch and Muriel Spark on *The Little Girls*, particularly for their interest in "nightmare and fantasy," and to Elizabeth Bowen's plan to write this novel "externally," without revealing her characters' thoughts and feelings. These are symptoms of a predicament. She was a novelist who had begun to write under the shadow of Forster and Virginia Woolf, whose affinities, in manner and subject, were with L. P. Hartley, Henry Green, Rosamond Lehmann and early Greene, and who found herself in the sixties at odds with her own methods. As her interest in the unconscious and the abnormal increased (the last two novels are concerned with involuntary recall, nonverbal communication, retardation, infantalism and fantasy life), so the controlled Jamesian analysis of motive and emotion began to seem inappropriate. As her environment became increasingly inimical to her, so the intense, nostalgic evocation of place at which she excelled, was put at risk. The last two novels are trying for a new kind of fictional language and method, but they succeed only in conveying qualms about the novel form itself. In the context of English fiction of the sixties they lack the solidity of the realists, and the wit and density of the "fabulists" who most influenced her.

All three of the late novels are preoccupied with time and recollection. They make similar references to *déjà vu* and to the overlap between memory and fantasy: "Were there not those who said that everything *has* already happened, and that one's lookings-forward are really memories?" "They say—don't they?—one never is doing anything for the first time." "Imagining oneself to be remembering, more often than not one is imagining: Proust says so. (Or is it, imagining oneself to be imagining, one is remembering?)" In the last two books retrospection is confused: there's some uncertainty as to what actually has happened. *A World of Love,* however, is poignant and idyllic in its pursuit of the past. As the extravagant title implies (taken from Traherne's "There is in us a world of Love to somewhat, though we know not what in the world that should be"), it is a romance of feelings and personal relations, in retreat from the wider political reverberations of *The Heat of the Day.* It is also as close to being a ghost story as her novels were ever allowed to come—and might, perhaps, have worked better as a long short story in the manner of "The Happy Autumn Fields," with which it has affinities.

From the start of the novel—County Cork, the sun rising ("on the heat of the day before") for an exceptionally hot June day, an "expectant, empty, intense" landscape, a dilapidated house, Montefort, "somewhat surprisingly" fronted by an obelisk, a beautiful girl of twenty in a "trailing Edwardian muslin dress" coming out to read a letter—the atmosphere is so characteristic as to be almost self-parodic. Like "The Happy Autumn Fields," the novel initially gives the impression of being set in the past. And, like that story, it cuts roughly and abruptly to the squalid modern litter of a bedroom inside the house: "a packet of Gold Flake, a Bible, a glass with dregs, matches, sunglasses, sleeping pills, a nail file and a candlestick caked with wax into which the finished wick had subsided." Evidently Montefort's hand-to-mouth condition in the fifties is to be contrasted with the past and the rapt romanticism of the girl reading the letter is to be matched against the disabused toughness of the woman asleep in the bedroom. Characters, setting and plot are thoroughly Bowenesque. For all its flaws, *A World of Love* is a touching novel, in being, as it transpired, a farewell to the Irish subject and to many of her familiar materials.

Like Henrietta and Leopold uncovering the past of the house in Paris, Jane Danby's find of a bundle of letters in the trunk with the dress unlocks the past of Montefort. As with the two children in the earlier novel, her chance discovery not only raises ghosts but liberates her into her own future. The story of the sleeping princess, as in other works, is invoked, but in this case the heroine is not awakened for a tragic shock or disillusionment, like Lois, Emmeline, or Portia. *A World of Love* is the most benign of the novels.

But, like *The House in Paris,* it does contain an unhappy past, which has produced the uneasy circumstances of the life at Montefort. Antonia, the woman in the bedroom, has been the owner of the house since her cousin, Guy (the writer of the letters), died in the war in 1918. At his death, Guy was engaged to an English girl, Lilia, then a beautiful and bewildered seventeen-year-old. Antonia took charge of Lilia's life, to the extent of marrying her off at thirty to another cousin, the "wild," illegitimate Fred Danby, and of installing the couple at Montefort. There, the marriage worked itself out through stages of passion and coldness, two children were born, Jane and her eccentric younger sister, Maud, and the Danbys' ill-defined status as "caretakers," farmers and hosts to Antonia continued for twenty-one years, due to the reluctance to "sitting down and having anything out." Lilia's brooding dislike of Montefort and of Antonia, Fred's dotage on his elder daughter, the estrangement of husband and wife, and Antonia's nerve-wracked impatience with the whole set-up are ignited by Jane's discovery of Guy's letters. Thirty or more years on, he seems to return, as the letters fall into the hands of every member of the household. Jane falls in love with her idea of him; the emotion translates her from a girl to a woman. Spotted as a rising beauty by the neighbouring châtelaine, "Lady Latterly," at the local fête, she goes to a dinner-party at the castle—a comic setting which the ghostly presence of Guy (who must often have dined there with the past owners) transforms into a bridal feast. Jane moves into Lady Latterly's orbit, and is driven by the castle chauffeur to Shannon airport, to meet one of Lady Latterly's guests—and cast-off boyfriends—Richard Priam. The time is right, the letters have prepared the ground: "They no sooner looked but they loved."

This romantic movement is counterpointed, with characteristic wryness, by the antic "possession" of Maud, struggling with her "familiar," laying curses on her family, and racing to the radio to listen to the strokes of Big Ben, and by the disconcerting effect of the letters on the older generation, now (like Elizabeth Bowen) in their fifties. Antonia's painful love of Guy, Fred and Lilia's jealousy and bitterness are re-enacted; all are haunted by the writer of the letters, who, it transpires, has been unfaithful to both women. But, unlike *The House in Paris* and *To the North,* and like *The Death of the Heart,* this is a novel of compromise, not of tragedy. Lilia and Fred move towards a more companionable relationship, Antonia belatedly accepts Guy's love for Lilia and her own necessary bond with her. Though "one was never quite quit of what one has done," by the end of the novel the ghost has been exorcised, and "the future was the thing."

If *A World of Love* is arrived at after the earlier works, its ghostliness can be seen to arise partly from the self-referential echoes. These don't merely consist of general resemblances—to the structure of the past breaking in on the present, as in *The House in Paris* or "The Happy Autumn Fields," to the pattern of relationships in *The Death of the Heart* (Antonia and Jane mildly re-enact the hostilities between Anna and Portia), or to the subject of *The Last September,* a young girl waiting for something to happen in an Irish house. There are more specific allusions. Maud is a compound of Elizabeth Bowen's most horrible small girls. Lilia remembering her farewell to Guy at the railway station, where she overheard him speaking intimately to Antonia, calls up a scene very like the embrace between Karen and Max on the train at Victoria. What Lilia hears Guy saying is "You'll never see the last of me!" The words recall the parting of the soldier in "The Demon Lover": "I shall be with you," he said, "sooner or later. You won't forget that. You need do nothing but wait." Jane's visit to Lady Latterly's castle is like Marianne's excursion with Davina in "The Disinherited." Like Marianne, Jane moves in a rapt, ethereal trance through the "void, stale, trite and denying drawing-room"; like the thirties socialites in "The Disinherited," Lady Latterly's English guests are ghostlike: there was "something phantasmagoric about this circle of the displaced rich." *A World of Love* is haunted by its author's past creations, and most of all by the earlier books and stories about Anglo-Ireland.

When *A World of Love* is set against the Anglo-Irish novel of 1929, its shadowiness is apparent. Although *The Last September* was set back in the time of the Troubles, and although the courtship of Lois and Gerald was romantically treated, the early novel was much more full-blooded than *A World of Love*. Lois was, after all, in love with a real soldier, and not the ghost of one. Anglo-Irish society, though diminished, was still felt to possess energy and decorum; and the individual lives were inextricably related to the political situation. In *A World of Love* the girl is in love with a phantom, there is no Anglo-Irish society, and the lives at Montefort and at the castle, lives of demeaning poverty or demeaning wealth, exist in a vacuum. For all that the novel describes a dreamy prelude to adult love, its real subject is loss. This is the last, faint, spectral chapter in the history of Anglo-Ireland.

Thus the novel's successes are not the romantic set-pieces—Jane sensing Guy's presence opposite her at the castle dinner-party, Antonia and Lilia pursuing their memories of Guy—but its wry accounts of what has become of the Anglo-Irish and their homes. The English Lady Latterly, of dubious past, who has bought up "an unusually banal Irish castle, long empty owing to disrepair" is part of an influx of *nouveau riche* moving in on a landscape once "vigilant" against newcomers, and scattered with "eyeless towers and time-stunted castles." To one old Irish guest, who remembers County Cork, as it used to be, she and her friends are no substitute for the real society they have replaced: "You can buy up a lot; you can't buy the past . . . these days, one goes where the money is—with all due respect to this charming lady. Those days, we went where the people were."

The castle's money is good enough for the local shopkeepers, however, who have been known to stop Montefort's credit. Again, a comparison between this depressing town, and the liveliness of Mrs Fogarty's Clonmore drawing-room in *The Last September,* shows the decline:

> There on the kerb outside Lonergan's, Lilia braced her shoulders as though facing reality—looking up then down the Clonmore straight wide main street at the alternately dun and painted houses, cars parked askew, straying ass-carts and fallen bicycles. Dung baked on the pavements since yesterday morning's fair; shop after shop had insanely similar doorways, strung with boots and kettles and stacked with calicoes—in eternal windows goods faded out. Many and sour were the pubs. Over-exposed, the town was shadeless—never a tree, never an awning. Ice cream on sale, but never a café. Clonmore not only provided no place to be, it provided no reason *to be,* at all.

Montefort (based on a deserted farmhouse near Bowen's Court but with much of the atmosphere of Bowen's Court itself) has, like a house in a Somerville and Ross novel, "the air of having gone down." The obelisk was built by a typical Anglo-Irish landlord:

> "Married the cook . . . went queer in the head from drinking and thinking about himself, left no children—anyway, no legits. So this place went to his first cousin."

Now it is isolated ("no calls to the telephone for there was not a telephone, no vans delivering, seldom a passer-by, no neighbours to speak of") and decrepit:

> The green of the ivy over the window-bars and the persisting humidity of the stone-flagged floors made the kitchen look cool without being so. This was the room in Montefort which had changed least: routine abode in its air like an old spell. Generations of odours of baking and basting, stewing and skimming, had been absorbed into the lime-washed walls, leaving wood ash, raked cinders, tea leaves, wrung-out cloths and lamp oil freshly predominant. The massive table, on which jugs had been

danced at the harvest homes, was probably stronger than, now, the frame of the house . . . The great and ravenous range, of which no one now knew how to quell the roaring, was built back into a blackened cave of its own—on its top, a perpetual kettle sent out a havering thread of steam, tea stewed in a pot all day, and the lid heaved, sank on one or another of the jostling pots, saucepans or cauldrons. Mush for the chickens, if nothing else, was never not in the course of cooking . . . The sink's one tap connected with a rain-water tank which had run dry—since then, a donkey cart with a barrel rattled its way daily down to the river pool . . . On the dresser, from one of the hooks for cups, hung a still handsome calendar for the year before; and shreds of another, previous to that, remained tacked to the shutter over the sink. These, with the disregarded dawdling and often stopping of the cheap scarlet clock wedged in somewhere between the bowls and dishes, spoke of the almost total irrelevance of Time, in the abstract, to this ceaseless kitchen.

The passage illustrates what is excellent in the novel—this is a fully realized room—and what is exasperating. "Mush for the chickens was never not in the course of cooking" is a ludicrous piece of self-derived mannerism. The paragraph is full of similar affectations: the obtrusive placing of commas and of words like "now," the coy adjectival phrases like the "perpetual" kettle and the "ceaseless" kitchen, the obligatory inversions, qualifications, and double negatives. In its striving for a heightened poetical mood the novel relies heavily on these familiar tricks of style: "All round Montefort there was going forward an entering back again into possession"; "Decay . . . was apparent—out it stood! Nothing now against it maintained the place."

The manner blurs events and relationships. Fred's absorption with Jane, Antonia's brutal treatment of Lilia, Jane's attraction to Vesta Latterly, all promising studies of influence, are hazily rendered, especially if compared with, say, Thomas and Anna Quayne's marriage, or Leopold's encounter with Mme Fisher. Maud, venomously Protestant and covered in boils, a horrid embodiment of "moral force," is an exception, but she works as a parody of the haunted adults, and, in her obsession with Big Ben, as a convenient reminder of "the absolute and fatal" stroke of time. By contrast, the characterization of Jane is particularly soft and conventional: "Her brows were wide, her eyes an unshadowed blue, her mouth more inclined to smile than in any other way to say very much—it was a face perfectly ready to be a woman's, but not yet so, even in its transcendancy this morning."

Yet the novel does deal in ideas about time and memory which relate it to her better work. Jane's resistance to "the time she was required to live in," her aversion to the past's "queeringness"—"this continuous tedious business of received grievances, not-to-be-settled old scores"—is set ironically against the older generation's inability to free itself from the dead. The character most like the narrator, Antonia, is made to contemplate poignantly the effect of the wars on our response to death, and the postwar sense of unreality. This central passage explains and to some extent justifies the novel's shadowy, precious attenuations:

> Life works to dispossess the dead, to dislodge and oust them. Their places fill themselves up; later people come in; all the room is wanted . . . Their being left behind in their own time caused estrangement between them and us, who must live in ours.
>
> But the recognition of death may remain uncertain, and while that is so nothing is signed and sealed. Our sense of finality is less hard-and-fast; two wars have raised their query to it. Something has challenged the law of nature: it is hard, for instance, to see a young death in battle as in any way the fruition of a destiny, hard not to sense the continuation of the apparently cut-off life, hard not to ask, but *was* dissolution possible so abruptly, unmeaningly and soon? . . . These years she went on living belonged to him, his lease upon them not having run out yet. The living were living in his lifetime . . . They were incomplete.

Almost ten years elapsed before the next novel. The only intervening work, written at a very low point in Elizabeth Bowen's life, was *A Time in Rome* (1960), too personal and erratic to be a successful guide book, too impressionistic for a historical study. It contains, however, some characteristic remarks about time and memory which point towards the last novels:

> It is in nature (at least in mine) to make for the concrete and particular, to "choose" a time and reconstitute, if one can, one or another of its moments . . . In Rome I wondered how to break down the barrier between myself and happenings outside *my* memory. I was looking for splinters of actuality in a shifting mass of experience other than my own. Time is one kind of space; it creates distance. My chafing geographical confusion

was in a way a symptom of inner trouble—my mind could not
be called a blank, for it tingled with avidity and anxieties: I was
feeling the giddiness of unfocused vision. There came no help
from reason, so I was passive . . . To talk of "entering" the past
is nonsense, but one can be entered by it, to a degree.

The idea of being passively entered into by the past is derived from Proust,
who has always interested Elizabeth Bowen. She quotes him at the start of
The Last September, the first novel of time recalled. He is invoked in "The
Mulberry Tree," her 1934 account of her third English school, Downe
House, which is (partly) the school in *The Little Girls:* "Memory is, as
Proust has it, so oblique and selective that no doubt I see my schooldays
through a subjective haze." Eva Trout refers to Proust's idea of the overlap
between imagination and memory; and in the last collection, *Pictures and
Conversations,* there is a long, careful and penetrating essay on Proust's
novelist-character, Bergotte. *The Little Girls* is the most "Proustian" of her
novels: it describes an involuntary recall of the past, and the breakdown set
in motion by that recall. The novel not only contains a Proustian experience,
it produced one: when she began her draft of an autobiography in the
seventies, she said that she had "completely forgotten" one of her schoolgirl
experiences "till it was returned to me by *The Little Girls.*"

In one way, then, *The Little Girls* marks the culmination of a central
preoccupation, the uncontrollable activity of memory and the disabling
legacy of the past. She has, of course, set stories in the past before (*The Last
September*) or re-entered the past in the middle of a novel or story, as in *The
House in Paris* (which has the same structure as *The Little Girls*), "The
Happy Autumn Fields," *A World of Love,* and "Ivy Gripped the Steps," a
story rather like this novel. The central section of *The Little Girls,* which
describes schooldays at "St. Agatha's, Southstone," invokes the factual account of her schools in "The Mulberry Tree," and the many characteriza-
tions of schoolgirls, like Theodora Hirdman at Mellyfield in *Friends and
Relations,* or Pauline and her friend Dorothea in the "Going to School"
chapter of *To the North,* or the girl haunted by "the Crampton Park School
Tragedy" in "The Apple Tree." She says in "Pictures and Conversations"
that "St. Agatha's is imaginary, in that it has no physical origin." But she
admits that it runs together features from her three English schools, Lindum
House, her Folkestone day-school; Harpenden Hall, a Hertfordshire boarding school (where, as one of a series of "crazes," "a smallish biscuit tin,
sealed, containing some cryptic writings and accompanied by two or three
broken knick-knacks, was immured in the hollow base of a rough stone wall

dividing the kitchen garden"), and Downe House, her wartime Kentish boarding school, where the girls cultivated "foibles and mannerisms" in the interests of social success, and "personality came out in patches, like damp through a wall."

On either side of the novel's central section, the flashback to the three girl friends at school in 1914, are the two parts set in the sixties. Dinah Delacroix is a well-preserved, eccentric widow living in a Somerset villa, its garden lush with flowers and vegetables, in the company of her vain, temperamental, nosy house-boy, Francis (a faint reworking of Eddie) who waits (and spies) on Dinah while deciding what to do with his future, and her loyal simple old friend Frank Wilkins (a faint reworking of Major Brutt, and drawn, presumably, from Alan Cameron). The novel opens with Dinah embarked on her latest "craze": burying evidence for posterity in a cave.

> "Clues to reconstruct *us* from. Expressive objects. What really expresses people? The things, I'm sure, that they have obsessions about."

As she and Frank haphazardly go about this whimsical task, a neighbour's question ("Who's going to seal it up?") and the sight of a crooked swing in the garden suddenly ignites Dinah's memory:

> "I've been having the most extraordinary sensation! Yes, and I still am, it's still going on! Because, to remember something all in a flash, so completely that it's not 'then' but 'now,' surely *is* a sensation, isn't it? I do know it's far, far more than a mere memory! One's right back into it again, right in the middle . . . They say—don't they?—one never is doing anything for the first time."

Fifty or so years before, she and two other "little girls"—"Dicey," "Mumbo," and "Sheikie"—also buried evidence for posterity in a coffer in the school garden. Ignoring Frank's sensible warning ("Can't you see, they're not there any more!") Dinah is fired with the desire to summon her two friends and to dig up the treasure: "We are posterity, now." Her obsession sets in motion a comedy of reappearances and recognitions. Sheikie, "Southstone's wonder, the child exhibition dancer" has become the respectable Mrs Sheila Artworth, wife of a Southstone estate agent, once a much-bullied little boy whom Dinah last remembers as stuck inside a drainpipe at a picnic. Mumbo, the clumsy, clever child of an unhappy marriage, is now Clare Burkin-Jones, owner of "MOPSIE PYE chain of speciality giftshops," operating "throughout the better-class London suburbs and outward into the Home Counties."

The first part, in which Dicey brings about the reunion, is farcical, full of little fragmentary surprises and revelations, ending with Sheikie's news that St. Agatha's no longer exists: it was bombed in the Second War. The flashback of the second part to 1914 has a softening, mellowing effect on the novel. The suppressed romantic feeling between Dicey's beautiful, un-worldly mother (whose husband killed himself before Dicey was born) and Mumbo's father, the sad, handsome Major, is tenderly touched upon, and the schoolgirl comedy (poetry recitations, swimming lessons, the visit of a suffragette aunt, shopping for a chain to go round the coffer in Southstone's picturesque old High Street, the end-of-term picnic) is nostalgically ideal-ized, very much in the manner of the prewar South Coast scenes in "Ivy Gripped the Steps" (where Mrs Nicholson's relationship with the Admiral, and her refusal to believe in the coming war, anticipate this part of *The Little Girls*):

> Summer evening concerts began in the Pier Pavilion, which like a lit-up musical box admired itself in the glass of the darkening mauve sea; above, the chains of lamps along the Promenade etherealized strollers in evening dress, from the big hotels, bright-ghostly baskets of pink geraniums and the fretwork bal-conies they were slung from.

The partings on the beach at the picnic between Dicey's mother and the Major, and between Dicey and Mumbo, just before the outbreak of war, are poignantly done. This, and the chilling account of the Major's home-life (his wife, another Mrs Kelway, "successfully cauterized her loved ones"), are much the best things in the novel, and have the haunting quality of a good short story. Elizabeth Bowen's potent memories of her childhood in En-gland alone with her mother are once again put to good use here.

The jerky, comical tone associated with the present day is resumed in the third part, for the farcical night-time scene in which the three women dig up the coffer from what is now the back garden of a typical Bowenesque villa, Blue Grotto. The coffer is empty. After this discovery, Dinah breaks down; "Nothing's real any more." The last part of the book, in which Sheila and Clare, Frank, and Dinah's grown-up sons (with little girls of their own) look after the invalid, becomes increasingly sombre. The unhappiness of the two other women is revealed: Sheila, her dancing come to nothing, had, before her marriage, a clandestine affair with a sick man whom she left on his deathbed; Clare, whose marriage was "a mess," has never quite recovered from her childhood passion for Dinah's mother—but will not answer the question "Are you a Lesbian?" Behind their conventionally unhappy stories lies the even more clichéd fate of the romantic, undeclared lovers of the last generation: Clare's father fell at Mons, Dinah's mother died in the outbreak of Spanish 'flu at the end of the war. Until now, Dinah is the only person in the novel who has avoided pain. The others accuse her of cheating:

> "All your life, I should think, you have run for cover. 'There's Mother!' 'Here's my nice white gate!' Some of us have no cover, nothing to run to. Some of us more than *think* we feel."

Dinah is made to pay for her self-protective infantalism by the sense of nullity which now comes upon her. In the last part of the book she becomes a kind of visionary commentator on the hollowness of contemporary life:

> "There's a tremendous market for prefabricated feelings. . . . And I'll tell you one great centre of the prefabricated feeling racket, and that is, anything to do with anything between two people: love, or even sex . . . So many of these fanciful ways people have of keeping themselves going, at such endless expense of time and money, seem not only unneccessary but dated."

Her breakdown is an interesting attempt at a study of alienation, which reveals Elizabeth Bowen's own current unease as a novelist. Dinah's disorientation impells her to raise the question of the value of art: if the past has gone, any attempt to recapture it, like her own pursuit of the coffer, must be a lie. A bad watercolour of the old Southstone High Street, which has itself long since disappeared, provokes this outburst:

> "Something has given the man the slip, so in place of what's given him the slip he's put something else in . . . It might be better to have no picture of places which are gone. Let them go completely."

The statement points to the vacuum at the centre of *The Little Girls*.

The novel has used as its *donnée* the Proustian plot of the past being given back through the action of involuntary memory working through association. And other perceptible acknowledgments of *A la recherche* accompany this central idea. Elizabeth Bowen tries for Marcel's sense that he lives "surrounded by symbols" by introducing, not very tactfully, symbolic props: the objects placed in the original coffer, which include a revolver (to be used more melodramatically in *Eva Trout*); a butterknife with a gnarled thumb-shaped handle bought by Dinah from "MOPSIE PYE"; three grotesque masks made by a local craftswoman; and the china objects which used to clutter Dinah's mother's cottage and which are, for Clare, "a fragile representation of a world of honour, which is to say unfailingness."

The failure of that world reflects Proust's dictum that "the true paradises are the paradises that we have lost." The novel also pursues Proust's interest in what goes on in the mind in sleep, and in the self-forgetfulness necessary for refinding oneself. And the abortive re-encounters between the three women—particularly the adult confrontation between Dicey and Mumbo—conform to the pattern of disenchanting confrontations in Proust's novel, one of which Elizabeth Bowen describes in her essay on Bergotte: "A relationship . . . anticlimactic, patchy, uninspirational—a relationship haunted by what it should have been."

But, as she points out, "a magnified Bergotte exists on another plane." The disappointments of social intercourse, the inevitable failure of love (since we love only what we don't possess or have lost) are redeemed in *A la recherche,* by what Elizabeth Bowen describes as "The notion of purgation, of self-redemption, of brought-back virtue being possible for the artist by means of art." This concept of redemption through art—which is the whole point of Proust's novel—is entirely lacking from *The Little Girls.* In Elizabeth Bowen's novel art is seen as a lessening of experience rather than its justification: there is no route out of disappointment and dispossession. Her negation of Proust's idea is reflected in the difference of style: *The Little Girls* is not at all Proustian in the way it is written. Roger Shattuck says well of Proust's method that "As his novel tenaciously aims at assimilating the whole meaning of life, so each sentence strives to digest its whole subject." Exactly the opposite effect is produced by the style of *The Little Girls.* The "whole meaning of life" is held at arm's length; such "meaning" as there is appears in fragmentary and diffused form and is presented in a manner which is without depth or resonance. Not only does the novel record an unlikely and whimsical situation, which is dressed up with awkward attempts at comedy, uneasy ventures into symbolism and contrived literary allusions (mostly to *Macbeth,* in order that the three "revenants" should seem like the three witches—Sheikie even had a sixth toe at birth), but it also feels dubious and illusive.

Elizabeth Bowen has decided, at this point, to forgo the controlled, elaborate commentary and the sharp, minute, inward presentation of character which her earlier novels displayed. This narrative has, from the start, a provisional, indeterminate air, as my italics in this passage suggest. A man and a woman are carrying objects into a space in the ground:

This was, *if anything*, on the large and deep side . . . Across the
uneven rock floor, facing the steps, was *either* a shallow cave *or*
a deep recess—or, *possibly*, unadorned grotto? . . . A woman,
intent on what she was doing to the point of a trance, *could be
seen* in back-view . . . *She may not have heard* the man, who was
wearing espadrilles—she did not, *at any rate*, look round.

The dialogue these two embark on is brusque, jerky, and flatly colloquial:
"Oh, bother you," she grumbled, "do put your *specs* on!"—and the commentary on it is casually banal: "This was Frank's cue for another repeat-
remark." Though a few familiar baroque mannerisms linger on ("To put it
would all be going, before long") the first chapter establishes a deliberately
diminished and vapid level of prose. Although the flashback allows for a
more lyrical, alluring manner to insinuate itself ("From across the shrinking
watery miles came an expiring sigh—not like the sound of wind, a sigh in itself"), all three sections are characterized by cumbersome techniques, which
suggest an insecure search for a new method. There is the naming of people
by their activities, as in "said the willing learner," or "the maker-free then
threw open the window" or "sang out the homecomer." There's the equivocal commentary, as in "Yet she faltered, if for less than an instant, or just
barely—how rarely?—overrode a misgiving." And there's the preponder-
ance of thin, banal dialogue:

> "I wondered whether you'd telephone."
> "Well, I didn't."
> "No.—Last night, when *I* rang up, you sounded so cross."
> "You made me jump, suddenly coming through like that."
> "That's the worst of telephones. What were you doing?"
> "Well, I was in my flat."
> "Of course you were, else you couldn't have answered. What
> were you doing?"
> "Thinking about you," said Clare crossly.

These late techniques are not, I think, merely failures of assurance—
though they are those. They suggest that she was becoming increasingly
concerned with the concept of a breakdown in language. That Elizabeth
Bowen's highly charged, contrived and controlled style should have been
reduced to the clumsy procedures of *The Little Girls* can be attributed to
more than obvious reasons of old age and a dissatisfaction with outdated
formulae. The last two novels incorporate the idea of a future without any
verbal "style" at all. When the three schoolgirls bury their most precious

possessions in the coffer with a proclamation written in Mumbo's invented "Unknown Language," they ask each other whether it matters that posterity won't understand them:

> "And it may all be the same, by then? They may have no language."

The idea of a future without language is even more pronounced in the last novel, *Eva Trout,* which, though of interest as an illustration of Elizabeth Bowen's late *malaise,* provides an unfocussed and bizarre conclusion to her *opus.* The heroine, who is twenty-four at the start of the novel, is a recognisable type of "displaced person": she recalls Annabelle in "The Last Night in the Old Home" ("Inside the big, bustling form of a woman she was a girl of ten") and Valeria Cuffe, the demented heiress in "Her Table Spread," "abnormal—at twenty-five, of statuesque development, still detained in childhood." Like those unmanageable innocents, Eva Trout, an orphaned heiress, has peculiar habits. She stammers, is incapable of weeping, cannot behave with normal indifference or self-protectiveness, takes obsessional delight in certain objects (her car, her audio-visual machines), is large and ungainly, and has "a passion for the fictitious for its own sake." Her distraction is matched, as with all Elizabeth Bowen's most unworldly characters, by "the patient, abiding encircling will of a monster, a will set on the idea of belonging and of being loved." "I remain gone. Where am I? I do not know—I was cast out from where I believed I was," Eva complains. Her need to compensate for these feelings makes her dangerous: "You plunge peoples' ideas into deep confusion . . . You roll round like some blind indestructible planet."

Though she first appears in rural, homely circumstances—driving the vicar's wife and children in her Jaguar to look at a castle which used to be her school—it becomes apparent that she is out of touch with reality and attracts violence. Her family history is squalid and dramatic. Her father was a "popular" businessman who "deviated," running off with the "wicked" Constantine Ormeau. Her mother was killed in a plane crash with her lover, just after Eva's birth. Twenty-three years later, her father committed suicide. Eva, left on Constantine's hands, considers that he has murdered both her parents.

Her oddness is mainly attributed to this macabre history, but also to her disjointed education. For a time she attended the dubious experimental school at the castle (a "Bavarian fantasy" on the Welsh border) bought by her father as a means of getting rid of Constantine's other "friend," Kenneth, whose authority over the school's rich little delinquents (wittily sketched) came to an abrupt end. At this school Eva has a passion for a wraith-like child called Elsinore. After being dumped at various temporary international homes, Eva asked to go to an "ordinary" girl's school, where she fell in love with the brilliant young English teacher, Iseult Smith. At the start of the novel Eva is living with Iseult and her husband Eric Arble, whose shaky marriage, which has involved the end of her career and the compromise of his (from fruit farming to a garage) is weakening under Eva's demanding presence.

The random history of Eva's temporary homes and thwarted affections emerges patchily, not through Eva's thoughts but through information provided by other characters, and through an equivocal narrative which seems as much intent on obscuring characters and events as on establishing them. The fragmentary effect is sustained by a plot which jumps with deliberate waywardness through a series of unlikely journeys and settings: the novel's subtitle is "Changing Scenes." Feeling betrayed by Iseult, Eva moves away from the Arbles and the neighbouring vicarage to a huge, gloomy, baroque villa (Cathay) on the South Coast at Broadstairs. (Both the vicar's family and the villa return Elizabeth Bowen, for the last time, to her Kentish childhood.) Eric visits her, and Eva leads Iseult to suspect them of an affair. Then Eva suddenly disappears to America (where she accidentally encounters Elsinore). Her journey there is recorded in the letter of a comical American professor who becomes infatuated with her on the plane, but never reappears. Eight years later she returns to England with an adopted eight-year-old deaf mute, Jeremy, to find that the Arbles have separated, one of the vicarage daughters, Louise, has died, Constantine is as bland and shady as ever, and the vicar's son Henry has grown up into an elegant Cambridge undergraduate, who becomes the last of Eva's grand, impractical passions. Her time is erratically divided between stays in London hotels, outings to Cambridge and the castle with Henry, and a journey to France in search of a cure for Jeremy, whom she leaves with the Bonnards, two married "environmentalist" doctors at Fontainebleau.

The preposterously haphazard "plot" culminates in a farcical melodrama on Victoria Station. Eva and Henry are embarking on a "mock" wedding journey (a scene staged, at her request, in payment for all her "longing in vain" for him), witnessed by all the novel's protagonists, when Jeremy comes running up with a revolver he's found in Eva's luggage (which in fact—it's a very clumsy piece of plotting—belongs to the Arbles) and shoots his "mother" dead. The violent ending has been anticipated not only by Eva's family history but also by a succession of drastic events—Louise's death; the abduction of Jeremy in London, from a sinister sculptress who is supposed to be minding him, by a "mystery" woman who turns out to be Iseult; a reckless car drive with Henry (reminiscent of the "last ride together" in *To the North*) and Jeremy's occasional fits of temper.

There is no radical departure here: these dramatic incidents arise from

Elizabeth Bowen's permanent interest in the havoc wreaked by innocence. Eva's, and Jeremy's, destructive influence is a grotesque version of the violent extremism of Emmeline or Portia. That these unworldly girls, desperately intent on having their affections returned, are as dangerous to the adult world as it is to them, is a recurrent idea which is caricatured in the double personality of Eva and her son. The nature of the enemy is also familiar, though Elizabeth Bowen is now, as in *The Little Girls,* more outspoken about her characters' sexuality: St Quentin was not described as a homosexual, but he shares Constantine's qualities of aesthetic curiosity and unscrupulousness. Again, there's the conflict between the innocent girl and the disabused older woman, though Eva and Iseult, unlike Portia and Anna, are close enough in age for their relationship (like that of Dinah and Clare) to bear the suggestion of a potential or thwarted love-affair. (Though Elizabeth Bowen deals very unsympathetically with homosexuals in *Eva Trout,* there's a clear expression of understanding for lesbian feelings in the last two novels.) The women's names suggest their roles: Eva, "cast out from where I believed I was" (the first section is called "Genesis"), Iseult the temptress, who "betrayed" Eva's hopes, "having led them on." As well as being victim and seductress, however, they present two versions of the same malaise. Eva, who cannot weep and would prefer not to be able to speak ("What is the object? What is the good?") asks the question: "What becomes of anyone's nature?" The more articulate and literary Iseult speaks of her deadened feelings ("I've undergone an emotional hysterotomy") and describes life as an "anti-Novel": no importance, no sensation, attaches to events. She herself has been trying to write a novel which was "still-born" and she arranges to meet Eva in Dickens's house at Broadstairs, a scene which provides an excuse for her to meditate enviously on his rich literature of "longing." The idea of dispossession, particularly in contrast with the Victorians, is again central.

A development from the usual methods, however, is felt in the haphazardness of the novel's plot and the sketchiness of its relationships. There are patchy attempts at depth of character: Henry's sardonic combativeness with his father, and Iseult's matching up to Constantine have potential. But, clearly, this isn't what now interests her. *Eva Trout* is the most schematic, as well as being the most disorganized, of her novels. Her liking for Forsterian "guardians" (like Mr Emerson and Mr Beebe in *A Room with a View*) has already been displayed in *The Death of the Heart.* In her last novel the interplay between good and evil angels is no longer suppressed beneath a realistic level: *Eva Trout* unabashedly presents itself as a fairy tale, with Eva as its spellbound princess. Its settings (the castle, Cathay), its names (Eva,

Iseult), and its arrangement of characters, all suggest this, quite apart from Eva's propensity for strange journeys, sudden appearances and fantastical inventions. The novel is full of guardians. At the start there's a contest of wills over Eva between Iseult and Constantine; towards the end there's a struggle for authority over Jeremy between Eva, Iseult, the sinister sculptress, and the wise Bonnards. There are even two men of God, Henry's father, stern but incapacitated by hay fever, and Constantine's latest friend, a suspect Anglican East End priest who "specialized in iniquity."

Of all these figures of authority, the French doctors, who reject "the horrible doctrine of Predestination" and speak wisely for happiness ("a matter of genius") and for love ("We are at its mercy, but not altogether") are the most convincing. But their belief in choice and self-improvement in the end has no bearing on the fated outcome of the relationship between Eva and Jeremy. This final act is presumably meant to be, to an extent, triumphant: Jeremy, the only character with the true authority, that of pure innocence, liberates Eva through his violent act from the world to which she is so ill-adapted. The novel doesn't make this point clearly, but certainly the wordless relationship between Eva and Jeremy is its most powerful subject.

Eva's alienation is a form of instability. Her inability to articulate, her fantasies, her dislocated sense of her own past ("Time, inside Eva's mind, lay about like various pieces of a fragmented picture") handicap her to the point of insanity. But the deaf-mute child, whose physical condition provides an image of Eva's alienation, seems, obscurely, to compensate for her abnormality, to make her seem normal. Like Eva, Jeremy doesn't want to speak; but unlike her, he feels no lack: "He would like to stay happy the way he is." Jeremy's inward contentment provides a queer, mirror-image of Eva's desolation.

> The effect was not so much of more intelligence as of a somehow unearthly perspicacity. The boy, handicapped, one was at pains to remember, imposed on others a sense that *they* were, that it was *they* who were lacking in some faculty.

When Jeremy and Eva are alone together in America they inhabit an "Eden" which is entirely innocent of words. Her attempts to have him cured are a betrayal of that state (analogous to Iseult's seduction of Eva through education). Jeremy's shooting of Eva is partly felt to be an involuntary revenge for the betrayal of what are earlier described as "the inaudible years":

> His and her cinematographic existence, with no sound-track, in successive American cities made still more similar by their con-

tinuous manner of being in them, had had a sufficiency which was perfect. Sublimated monotony had cocooned the two of them, making them as near as twins in a womb. Their repetitive doings became rites . . . They had lorded it in a visual universe. They came to distinguish little between what went on inside and what went on outside the diurnal movies, or what was or was not contained in the television flickering them to sleep. From large or small screens, illusion overspilled on to all beheld. Society revolved at a distance from them like a ferris wheel dangling buckets of people. They were their own. Wasted, civilization extended round them as might acres of cannibalized cars. Only they moved. They were within a story to which they imparted the only sense.

The references to the cinema recur at the end of the novel, which is made to seem like a scene in a film, with Jeremy as the "child star." Clearly, this is felt to be the art form of a posterity without language. As long as Jeremy and Eva are undivided, they have found the perfect means of entering the still innocent, still inheritable, speechless future. It's thus no accident, though the change of scene might look gratuitous, that this is the only one of her novels to be set partly in America, where the conditions of the future, such as the ascendancy of film over the novel, can be more immediately ascertained. The prospect of an entirely "visual universe" is not offered as entirely consolatory. But our present conditions, the novel suggests, can no longer be mastered or even registered by our language:

> "*Feel?*—I refuse to; that would be the last straw! There's too much of everything, yet nothing. Is it the world, or what? Everything's hanging over one. The expectations one's bound to disappoint. The dread of misfiring. The knowing there's something one can't stave off. The Bomb is the least. Look what's got to happen to us if we do live, look at the results! Living is brutalizing; just look at everybody!"

This last novel, as much in its unhappy struggle with its own language and structure as in its account of alienation, describes an almost unbearable present, with which the traditional novel of order and feeling can no longer deal.

HARRIET S. CHESSMAN

Women and Language
in the Fiction of Elizabeth Bowen

"But what story is true? Such a pity, I sometimes think, that there should have to be any stories. We might have been happy the way we were."

"Something has got to become of everybody, I suppose, Cousin Nettie."

"No, I don't see why. Nothing has become of me; here I am, and you can't make any more stories out of that."

(*The Heat of the Day*)

Elizabeth Bowen's fiction, like much modern fiction compels a recognition of the danger inherent in all fiction-making. Stories are, quite simply, untrue; they capture us, as they tried to capture Cousin Nettie, in their nets. Roderick's response, in this context, that "Something has got to become of everybody, I suppose," sounds weak. Yet Nettie's resistance to stories offers a problematic alternative. Nettie asserts a state of being, an essential unchangingness, inviolable by story; but what is this state of being? How is it to be defined? Who, finally, *is* "Cousin Nettie" except as this figure enters into some relationship, and by extension into the *relation* of some story?

Like all characters, Nettie literally owes her existence entirely to her author; she inhabits a story whether she wants to or not. One could say that the author gives her asylum, within the text—the text allows a space within itself for a critique of the text's own project—but it is also true that the text contains Nettie, just as the literal asylum, Wisteria Lodge, contains her. She

From *Twentieth Century Literature* 29, no. 1 (Spring 1983). © 1983 by Hofstra University Press.

is kept out of the larger picture. It is Roderick who occupies more textual space. Inheriting the ancestral home of Nettie's husband, attempting to fill the gaps in family stories and the family line, Roderick occupies the position of a believer and a participant in story—a position which coincides directly with his own assumption of authority as head of the family. Roderick's acceptance of history, in all its senses, clearly emerges out of his happy assumption of the power to author the continuing story he has inherited.

The dialogue between these two figures becomes paradigmatic of the struggle, within Bowen's fictions, between two stances toward story and language, which find expression as two differing narrative impulses. I wish both to explore this struggle, and to determine its connection with gender, because Bowen appears to point to such a connection, and because such an inquiry raises significant questions about women writers in their relation to their own authority as storytellers. I hope to suggest that Bowen, like many women writers, reveals a profound ambivalence toward her own powers of authorship, and that this ambivalence involves a sense of her betrayal of her own gender. Women, in Bowen's vision, are inherently outsiders to discourse, unless they turn traitor and defect to the other side.

Bowen defines two primary positions for women with regard both to narrative and to language. Certain women become objects of narration, in stories told by the primary narrators and by characters who act as narrators. Yet, as objects, these women tend to resist their forced entrance into narrative, and to desire the presence of another narrative form. Usually these figures are either silent or inarticulate, and point to a desire for a new language based on models of silent and symbiotic union—a desire which emerges in the work of many other modern women writers, especially Virginia Woolf. Other female figures, however, assume a place as author, or coauthor, of a story. These women, who become alter egos of the inarticulate female figures, have the capacity to author, through their mastery of language, these other women; yet often, as with Iseult's half-authoring of Eva in *Eva Trout,* such creation comes freighted with danger. To bring such resisters into full character could result in an end to the story as it has been written. It is precisely this fear that allows the female storytellers to gain control over their own monstrous alter egos, and to silence their attempts at resistance. The story, in any case, is not one's own. Such female "authors" are often characters themselves in other people's texts: Iseult is not only a "D. H. Lawrence reader," but a D. H. Lawrence character, and it stands to reason that her own narrative impulse might be suspect, or perhaps divided.

It is the relation between these two positions that structures Bowen's fiction. Usually, the positions are fleshed out quite clearly in the form of two primary female characters, who become representative of these two roles: storyteller and object of the story, "insider" and "outsider." The plot tends to be generated by the distance between these alter egos—the struggle which occurs as a result of their difference—and by this movement into or out of authorship.

What is at stake here is a radical schizophrenia, and one which holds particular significance for women. If it is true, as Luce Irigaray has suggested, that women have remained silent within discourse, and that to become a speaking or writing subject is by definition to become "the masculine," then an apparently unbridgeable gap exists between woman as subject and woman as object. To become a subject necessitates a loss of one's actual being, in a distortion and appropriation through language. A woman entering the symbolic becomes by the workings of this logic a masculine speaker, and in "speaking for" herself as woman, she participates in a masculine misprision and silencing.

Whether this model is "true" or not has certainly become an issue of debate, among feminist critics, but what is clear is that, regardless of its absolute truth, it makes some stunning appearances in the work of many women writers, and therefore seems to bear a significant relation to women's own experience of themselves. What emerges is the problematic of how women can produce their own stories, as subjects, without being "appropriated to and by the masculine." Bowen scatters her novels with female figures who not only resist the narratives they see around them, but who themselves have no language, and who therefore cannot generate other texts. These figures haunt her: they represent the unarticulated and inchoate femaleness which must in some sense be betrayed or at least abandoned, in the very act of entering language to tell stories.

And this femaleness, in Bowen's terms, is as silent as Irigaray would suggest. Apart from the apparent distinction between women with language and women without it, Bowen often hints at the larger silence all women share within culture. In *The Heat of the Day*, it is Stella (her name—already unoriginal—emerging, possibly, straight out of Sydney's poem) who, according to her inarticulate alter ego Louie, can "sp[eak] beautifully," yet who discovers the bonds of silence between women in the drawing room of Mount Morris. The conventions of the drawing room, both in life and in art, necessitate certain linguistic conventions: certain stories must be upheld, certain words must not be spoken. In fact, the words do not exist which might break the "deep silence" sustained by generations of "Ladies" (not "women" now). It is this bond of silence which forms the identification between Stella and Louie, or Anna and Portia in *The Death of the Heart*, or Iseult and Eva in *Eva Trout*, an identification which persists in spite of the gap between two apparently different discourses. Yet it is the refusal to recognize this bond of cultural and linguistic silence which causes the alienation and withdrawal of both the female "speakers" and the primary narrators.

Through silence, Nettie resists the story she has been built into: the story of the wife contained on her husband's estate, held within the four walls of his house. In another version of such resistance, Louie Lewis, in the same novel, struggles directly against language itself. Louie longs for a return to a state of being which requires no language; as she says, " 'At home where I used always to be there never used to be any necessity *to* say; neither was there with Tom, as long as they let him stop here. But look now—whatever *am* I to, now there's the necessity?' " Like most of her Bowen counterparts, Louie desires a symbiotic union with another, in which silence would become the medium of communication. Bowen defines this desire as a female one, no matter what the gender of the other figure within this union shifts to: the mother can give way to the man, but the model for this union lies in the bond of prelinguistic identification between a mother and daughter. At the end of the novel, with her own baby, she achieves such a union again.

Yet this opposing stance toward language and story comes riddled with ambivalence. Just as Nettie's retreat from story lands her in a static and nonsignificant world, a world cut off completely even from the view outside her one window, Louie's incapacity to use language forces her into a perpetual regression. She can gain no identity without the defining power of words. When confronted with people who *can* "say," she tries desperately to enter their world of language, because she recognizes words as her only key to a visible existence. Significantly, it is to Harrison, subtle and insinuating wielder of language, that Louie first attempts to speak: "her object was to feel that she, Louie, *was*. . . ." By talking she hopes to assert a "self" from which such talk can proceed.

The impossibility of articulateness, however, overwhelms her. To her friend Connie she confesses:

> "It isn't you only. It's the taking and taking up of me on the part
> of everyone when I have no words. Often you say the advantage
> I should be at if I could speak grammar; but it's not only that.
> Look the trouble there is when I have to only say what I *can* say,

and so cannot ever say what it is really. Inside me it's like being
crowded to death—and more of it all getting into me. I could
more bear it if I could only say."

Louie chafes within language's bounds. Her words sit awkwardly and clash
against each other, without the smooth structure of "grammar." Yet what is
this structure? The very way in which "grammar" begins to disintegrate
here could be said to point to the fictiveness of the structure of grammar
itself. Louie opens gaps in language. She serves to alienate us too from its
operations. We begin to feel, with her, the impossible gap between words
and their meanings which lies at the heart of signification. The ambiguity
and shiftiness of the referent intended by the word "it" in this passage
suggests the arbitrariness and uncertainty of referentiality. There is a sense
in which whatever the "it" refers to can never be spoken. The unarticulated
world which "crowd[s]" Louie "to death" is precisely that realm of experience which can find no place in language. And once one enters language, the
world one desired to make present is abandoned and perhaps betrayed.

Is it only Louie, and figures like her, then, who "cannot ever say what it
is really"? Is it just that she "ha[s] no words," or is it possible that the
referent, whatever it is, cannot be referred to with language and so be
communicated? Louie's speech here—and it stands out partly by being far
and away the longest speech that Louie ever makes, and the most abstract—
gains a resonance that goes further than Louie herself. It strikes a difficulty
at the core of this book, and of most of Bowen's work. Its resonance with
other speeches, by other figures who apparently occupy positions within
language, begins to suggest how the boundary between those inside and
those outside language or story can disintegrate into a common knowledge
of language's inadequacy. Justin, a writer, states in one of Bowen's short
stories, "Summer Night":

"We can no longer express ourselves: what we say doesn't even
approximate to reality; it only approximates to what's been said.
I say, this war's an awful illumination; it's destroyed our dark;
we have to see where we are. Immobilised, God help us, and
each so far apart that we can't even try to signal each other. And
our currency's worthless. . . . We've got to mint a new one. . . . I
taste the dust in the street and I smell the limes in the square and
I beat round inside this beastly shell of the past among images
that all the more torment me as they lose any sense that they
had."

Language, in Justin's view, is wholly mediated. It does not achieve a transparent union of signifier and signified, but veers instead toward a continual approximation of other signifiers. It remains self-contained and unreferential. "What's been said" stands in the way of any new saying. The writer's imagination becomes merely "this beastly shell of the past."

Yet such confessions, on the part of insiders, are rare. It is the function of the female characters outside the dominant discourse to undercut their alter egos' movement into language and story by pointing to the arbitrariness and inadequacy of these phenomena. It is precisely because of this deconstructive function that these figures are dealt with so ambivalently, by both the primary narrators and the storytelling characters: "Is she a snake or a rabbit?" as Anna says of Portia. These figures outside discourse, in their potential manifestation as "snakes," haunt the garden that writers, among others, cherish. Resisting stories, and resisting language, they uncover the scandal at the heart of authorship itself. In Edward Said's terms, they are occupied with molestation; they expose the shaky and fictive ground that writing rests on. And they suggest, as well, what might have been left out of "writing" as it has been.

Why, then, does Bowen give them breath? And why does she place them in a position of such tension with other female characters? I would suggest that they represent Bowen's own resistance to what she conceives to be the act of fiction-making, which serves to silence and to distort an experience primarily defined as female. A longing for another language, one of transparency and truthfulness, resides just to the side of this resistance. One could say that this desire is a traditional Romantic one for an absence of mediation, and it is romantic; yet Bowen defines it further as a peculiarly female desire. Her female "outsiders" blunder into the truth, despite, or perhaps because of, their bad "grammar." Because they stand outside the confines of linguistic convention, which is predicated upon an artificial distance between what is said and what is referred to, they appear to have the freedom to speak at least some of the "truth," even if they "cannot ever say what it is really." To be able to say "what it is really" would be to take this desire for truth to a longed-for but impossible extent: this truth and this reality are precisely what language as it is now structured cannot represent. Yet clearly these figures point the way. As Louie says: "Because *I* can't help what it sounds like; I speak the truth every time." And as the narrator observes: "Halted and voluble, this could be but a mouth that blurted rather than spoke, a mouth incontinent and at the same time artless."

The possibility for redemption, then, exists in the artlessness; yet what would the text look like that relied wholly on this lack of form? It is Bowen's own fear that allows these figures room—even rooms of their own—but doesn't allow them power, or certainly not enough power to crack the walls of convention completely, even if this were possible. These figures represent her own impulse toward a breaking of narrative form, yet her treatment of them, her containment of them, as a narrator and as an author, prevents the attempt to embody this impulse.

Bowen's own identification with these figures is represented in part by the identification other female characters experience. The alter egos of the resisters (Stella in *The Heat of the Day*, Celia in *To the North*, Anna in *The Death of the Heart*, Mrs. Kerr in *The Hotel*, or Iseult in *Eva Trout*) can also touch on the truth; such revelatory moments always occur in conjunction with a movement toward identification at some point in the text between these two female figures. Louie, in the same long speech referred to above, contrasts Stella's way of speaking with her own: "Now she tonight, she spoke beautifully: I needn't pity her—there it was, off her chest." Stella, at the moment Louie refers to her, speaks only to Louie; they have come together in a wholly accidental way—the man Harrison is the link that draws them into speech. Yet the very accidental nature of this encounter— the very improbability of it—suggests the presence of a bond between them which is hidden almost completely by the rest of the text.

The intricacy of their encounter bears examination: it becomes paradigmatic of the doubleness of the alter ego bond, for these two women experience both identification with and alienation from each other, in terms of their relation both to language in general and to the story in which they each find themselves. Louie's response to Harrison's language is what sparks the moment of dialogue between Louie and Stella: Harrison uses words to define both women. " 'What I saw you were, *and* are,' replied Harrison, 'is a pest. . . .' He looked at Stella and said: 'As for you, are you off your head? Do you think we have got all night?' " Louie reacts to this onslaught with a direct and artless cry: "No . . . how he can have the heart!" to which she adds, to Stella, "Oh, I wonder you go with him!" Louie protests Harrison's definitions, but at another level she could also be said to be protesting definition itself, for the distortion it imposes on its objects. Stella, by contrast, acts as apologist for Harrison. Opening her private dialogue with Louie, Stella says:

> "You mustn't mind his manner."
> "Don't you mind his manner?"
> "One cannot always choose."

> "I should have thought you should have had other chances,"
> said Louie lifelessly . . . "Though you ought not to mind me
> either," she had to add, "because I always do get upset; they say
> so."

"Manner" here suggests at first simply a surface mode of behavior; but its implications reach further. It touches closely upon convention itself, at both a social and a literary level. Harrison is "mannered": the form he participates in is both conventional and artificial. The configuration of the first three letters—"man"—may be wholly accidental, but, in conjunction with the masculine pronoun "his," the hint of gender here is unmistakable: this manner emerges from a man's world, which Stella attaches herself to and appears to accept, no matter how hard she fights it. The language she shares in with Harrison is opaque, indirect, censored, just as the language she exchanges with Robert, her lover, is predicated upon a silence: in the first moment of speech between Stella and Robert, their words are unheard, shattered by the detonation of a bomb. "What they *had* both been saying, or been on the point of saying, neither of them ever now were to know."

The dominant discourse in *The Heat of the Day,* then, as in most Bowen novels, becomes suspect for two primary reasons: its power of defining its objects, and thereby misrepresenting them; and its suppression of possible truth. A further question arises, however, as to the representability of this "truth" at all within language as it is arranged. When Stella, inspired by Louie's resistance to Harrison's language, attempts to identify with Louie and speak the truth, she resorts to a further indirection. Referring obliquely and with irony to the position Harrison has brought her to—she must submit to an affair with him if she wishes to prolong Robert's life—Stella states:

> "This evening was to have been a celebration, the first of many
> more evenings. It may still be the first of many more evenings,
> but what will they be worth? This is the truth," she said, looking
> round her at all the other people apprehensively staring into each
> other's faces. "He cannot bear it; let's hope he will forget it—
> let's hope that; it is the least we can do. We're all three human."

As Louie will later say, "there it was, off her chest": but what is the "it"? An astonishing absence of referentiality here—or perhaps an evasion of referentiality—undercuts the assertion of truth-telling. Syntactically, neither the "This" nor the "it" possess a signified object, unless the referent is precisely that "nothing" that remains unstated within the gap between the question and the apparent answer. The near quotation of T. S. Eliot's "Burnt Norton" raises a further problem: is Bowen, like Stella, or like Justin in "Summer Night," referring only to other art, other words? The possibility of a continual regression, from signifier to other signifier, gives further support to the possibility that "what it is really," as Louie would put it, can never be expressed.

Louie's response to this language of indirection, which Stella still participates in, marks one side of Bowen's own response. At first Louie is "overpowered" and literally paralyzed: she "heaved about on her chair as though bound by ropes to it." The language has power over her; it binds her in by its enforcement both of her silence (she does not speak during Stella's monologue) and, in a larger sense, of silence itself. Yet Louie "g[ets] herself free, st[ands] up," and asserts simply: "I ought to be getting back where I am." The oddity of Louie's language here represents her assertion of freedom from language's ordinary bounds: in breaking its code of convention she allows us the illicit hope that another language will be able to be found. *And* another subject, for another story: "she found, with a shock, that what she now most wanted was never to speak of [Harrison] again." "Already" "[a] fog of abhorrence" is "blotting out what he said." As potential storyteller, Louie substitutes, in place of Harrison, a female cast of characters: Stella without Harrison, Stella with Louie. As Anna will do at the end of *The Death of the Heart* with regard to her alter ego Portia, Louie imagines what Stella is like and gives her voice; yet what is odd is that now it is the inarticulate who imagines the articulate into existence. At the heart of the imagining is identification: Louie may feel herself "entered by what was foreign," yet this alienation is also a fusion. We are offered the possibility for a new story that will be composed of such fusions: in place of gaps, between characters or between signifiers and their significations, there will be a wholeness and a transparency. A genuine dialogue will replace a silencing monologue. Objects will not be captured and defined by words or by narrative, but will become subjects in their own right.

Yet this new language and new story remain problematic. Louie still cannot write this unwritten text. In her inspired musing on Stella, Louie sees "pictures" but no "words." The words she does come up with ("A soul astray") mark a sudden distancing from Stella as the object being defined through a rather artificial and timeworn synecdoche. Louie, like Portia or Eva Trout, avoids an assertion of power through definition as long as she stays away from language; yet how can their stories be told without the use of some language? In Louie's picturing of Stella, Stella becomes co-subject: no gap exists between subject and object. Yet Louie's "pictures" must be translated. The narrator acts as translator, but we must question the accuracy of the translation. To a large and disturbing extent, Louie's actual imaginings can never find adequate representation within language, and the possibility for a new language remains only in the realm of desire. Furthermore, the object of her imaginings eludes even her pictures, to the extent that this object occupies a realm of language inaccessible to Louie: " 'But this is not goodbye, I hope,' had been said—but what, how much, had she [Stella] meant to mean?"

Bowen's figures outside language, then, hint at possibilities for language and for story that remain unfulfilled. The power to represent and define rests with other characters, including both male characters and the female characters who stand as alter egos to their female counterparts outside. Such representation involves betrayal. As those with language become storytellers, they participate in the "overpowering" of inarticulate or silent objects which all authorship—at least in part—involves.

The Death of the Heart (1938) explores this question of authorship more directly than almost any other Bowen novel. It is no accident that one of the central characters, St. Quentin, is a novelist; and his vocation becomes in some sense diffused among the other characters, most of whom attempt to construct their own stories. Anna is one of the strongest "authors," and it is her sister-in-law Portia who becomes an unwitting and unwilling character in Anna's story.

Chapter 1 of the first book, "The World," can serve as a model for this dynamic: in it, Anna joins with St. Quentin in talk, the object of which is, of course, Portia. Although St. Quentin asks questions, and plays the part of responder, Anna's talk is essentially a monologue, not a dialogue, which gives us a clue as to the nature of her discourse: she occupies a position more of authority than of possible collaboration. This is not "gossip" of an educative and bond-creating kind: such gossip, as Patricia Meyer Spacks suggests, involves the participation of two intimate subjects who explore crucial issues through a discussion of an absent third. Anna and St. Quentin are involved less in attempting to establish their own intimacy (St. Quentin, in fact, "detested intimacy, which, so far, has brought him nothing but pain"), or to discover answers together, than in what Spacks terms "power," a third element of gossip: Anna seeks power over Portia by defining her. And she defines with a vengeance. As Anna begins, about the servant, Matchett:

> "You know what some servants are—how they ride one
> down, and at the same time make all sorts of allowance for
> temperament in children and animals."

"You would call her a child?"

"In ways, she's more like an animal. I made that room so pretty before she came. I had no idea how blindly she was going to live."

Further, this blind animal-like creature, according to Anna, "had made nothing but trouble since before she was born." Anna proceeds to tell her version of what she terms the "story" of Portia's birth, a narrative which takes up approximately ten pages and possesses a clear bias and deliberate shaping. Anna's storytelling becomes suspect partly through the fact that we hear this story again, in different forms, both in chapter 6, when Matchett retells it to Portia, and in chapter 2, when we have a sudden and unusual glimpse into Portia's own memory of her mother. Yet, no matter which way the story is told, Anna's version holds, to the extent that Portia's birth, and the circumstances of her birth, emerge as an unfortunate fall. Both Matchett's and Anna's versions converge on this point, and Portia is left imprisoned by her status within the story, as the accidental product of an illegitimate and rather ridiculous union. Portia attempts a revision of this ending: to Matchett she protests, "in a panic: 'But we were happy, Matchett. We had each other; he had Mother and me—Oh, don't be so angry: you make me feel it was my fault for having had to be born.'"

What is striking is that Anna is so often seconded, in her representation of Portia, by the narrator of *The Death of the Heart*, not only in the famous "innocence" passage, but throughout the text. In comparing Anna's response to the spring to Portia's, for example, the narrator clearly sides with Anna: "This was Portia's first spring in England: very young people are true but not resounding instruments. Their senses are tuned to the earth, like the senses of animals; they feel, but without conflict or pain." One may wonder how, after a story which has described precisely Portia's "conflict" and "pain," the narrator could suddenly simplify and distance this figure in a definition so resonant with Anna's earlier definitions. The narrator displays at various points in the text an ambivalence toward this creature who becomes the object of narration. The narrator, in fact, stands in the same double relation of identification and alienation to Portia as Anna does. While the narrator assumes such authority of definition, and thus of alienation, this authority becomes questioned by the continual sense that another side to the story may remain.

Portia's desire for her own language and story, like Louie's, then, undergoes a double treatment by the author. This object of so many stories attempts to become a subject in her own right. Significantly, it is her own text—her diary—that leads to Anna's long opening narrative. Portia's diary represents the characteristic Bowenesque yearning for a language which is transparent, not opaque, which contains the "truth," as opposed to the shadows and lies of the dominant discourse. Yet the model for such a language hints at the impossibility of its actual emergence: this desire, like Louie's, originates in silence. It is the memory of the utterly silent bond of communication which existed between her mother and herself that inspires Portia's need for a true language. Portia's first recorded memory, within the novel, is of ascending the crag in Switzerland with Irene, "arm-in-arm in the dark . . . pressing each other's elbows," as if within the womb-like "tent for the mind" created by the rain they can merge into each other bodily, and form one being, just as "arm-in-arm" forms one word. Everything they do is done together, often in "turn abouts." Even their wishes are wished to-gether, and at every point what they do or feel seems to be less spoken than understood perfectly before speech: "Untaught, they had walked arm-in-arm along city pavements, and at nights had pulled their beds close together or slept in the same bed—overcoming, as far as might be, the separation of birth."

Yet this desire for perfect communion, and for a language which could reproduce this communion, resembles Louie's "pictures": it loses in the translation. It can be imagined, but the narrative itself radically questions whether, given the nature of language, it can ever be reproduced. Portia's diary, as a private entity, may reach for a true language; yet, as St. Quentin points out, even Portia's first sentence shows "style." And "[s]tyle is the thing that's always a bit phony, and at the same time you cannot write without style. . . . And a diary, after all, is written to please oneself—there-fore it's bound to be enormously written up."

St. Quentin acts as counterpoint to Portia: the novelist points out the resemblances to his own art in an art which attempts to move beyond fiction. Pure fiction, according to his scheme, is safer than her kind; his novels attempt no referentiality, and so manage to avoid the truth entirely. As he puts it: "if one didn't let oneself swallow some few lies, I don't know how one would ever carry the past." Yet even though a diary appears to reproduce "facts," and so becomes dangerous, it too can never capture them fully, and perhaps, as St. Quentin suggests, the result can be even more treacherous:

> "You're working on us, making us into something. . . . You precipitate things. I daresay," said St. Quentin kindly, "that what you write is quite silly, but all the same, you are taking a liberty. You set traps for us. You ruin our free will."

"I write what has happened. I don't invent."

"You put constructions on things. You are a most dangerous girl."

"No one knows what I do."

"Oh, but believe me, we feel it. You must see how rattled we are by now."

"I don't know what you *were* like."

"Neither did we: we got on quite well then."

No act of writing, St. Quentin argues, can free itself of interpretation and distortion. Writing itself transforms what it desires to represent: it cannot present things wholly and transparently; it can only present *again*. This dialogue between St. Quentin, the novelist, and Portia Quayne, the diarist, bears a peculiar resonance which travels well beyond the situation at hand. Who is really speaking here? We are reminded that the novel in which this dialogue takes place, *The Death of the Heart*, is "working" on precisely the same characters as Portia's diary. Portia's words here, in defense of her own act of writing, could be Elizabeth Bowen's just as it is Bowen's own character, St. Quentin, who questions and accuses his author. None of us can know "what [these characters] *were* like," for Bowen's authoring of the characters, no matter what desires she originally had, has shaped them—changed them?—and other possibilities have been lost. What manifests itself here is a sense of guilt at the act of authorship itself, as well as a fear that no form of language or story can be found that isn't "distorted and distorting." "You are a most dangerous girl," Bowen could be saying, with some wryness, to herself. Portia is one of the few female characters who attempts to write, and who clearly attempts another form of writing. Her failure becomes by extension Bowen's failure, and the result is a troubled belief in the danger of attempting to write at all.

This guilt of authorship reappears with compelling force in Bowen's last completed novel, *Eva Trout, or Changing Scenes* (1968). The structure of authorship is intricate: two "authors" exist, Iseult and Eva, yet Eva has also been "authored" by Iseult, or at least half-authored. Such creation of an other—which in this book becomes defined as a female creation—is burdened with danger. It rests on the schizophrenia which I have been exploring throughout this essay: the division between the insider and the outsider, the figure who inhabits the world of language or story and the figure who remains somehow outside that world.

Eva Trout hovers between these two realms: she is both motherless and fatherless, a position which translates into linguistic terms. Like Louie or Portia, she longs for a symbiotic and silent union with another woman, a mother; her own mother died when she was three (presumably at the age when Eva left this world of pre-linguistic union), and she tries to re-create such a bond with another girl in adolescence. Significantly, this girl, Elsinore, is in a coma; "[t]his deathly yet living stillness, together, of two beings, this unapartness," which "came to be the requital of all longing," does not rely on active and separate identities. Identity, in fact, does not yet exist, for language does not exist. It is toward what appears to be a father-tongue that Iseult, Eva's second mother, pushes her. Iseult takes it upon herself to raise Eva up into language, to give her an identity within language. She asks Eva to attempt making connections and sequences out of her "cement-like" "conversational style": "try joining things together: this, then that, then the other."

Yet Iseult's very name gives us a glimpse into the nature of this father-tongue. She is above all a character herself, created in male texts. She reads not only D. H. Lawrence, but Henry James and Charles Dickens: it is in Dickens's house that she meets Eva at one point. She has also been a "teacher of English." Finally, she is allied with Eva's "guardian," Constantine, who becomes a part-author as well: he must "authorise" "any arrangement involving money" for Eva, and we are told that Eva's residence with Iseult "suited Constantine's book," as if, godlike (or emperor-like), he owns the book in which Eva's life is written. Even Iseult is on salary to him, and is dependent on his "authorisations."

It was presumably Eva's parents who named her; but it is Constantine who explains the name through his definition of Eva: "Eva's capacity for making trouble, attracting trouble, stewing trouble around her, is quite endless. She, er, begets trouble—a dreadful gift. And the more so for being inborn." The "trouble" this latter-day Eve "begets" apparently has to do with her relation to language, and, at a larger cultural level, to convention. Eva's language is "outlandish"—literally, it is from out of the land, not indigenous. She does not know how to speak English. She is named, and in the naming she is thrust into structures of language and convention extending as far back as the Bible (the first book of *Eva Trout* is entitled "Genesis"), yet she herself, because of her status outside the dominant discourse, does not participate in such naming, and, in fact, her position as outsider becomes one of a potentially freeing power. As Margaret Homans states in *Women Writers and Poetic Identity,* the biblical "Eve, and women after her, have been dislocated from the ability to feel that they are speaking their own language." Such dislocation, as Homans suggests, can be liberating for the woman writer, as it was for Emily Dickinson, if it leads to a satanic discovery that all discourse is not literal, but fictive. A suggestion hovers throughout *Eva Trout* that perhaps, if Eva had been brought fully into language by her teacher Iseult, the result might have been strangely disruptive of the linguistic world around her, which is so clearly fictive but which relies on its unquestioned sense of its own truthfulness. Iseult fears Eva as a potential Dickinsonian author, in Homans' terms. Yet the possibility for such freely duplicitous and deconstructive language is unrealized. Eva can barely articulate her own presence, and in fact seems to become trapped in conjugations of the primary verb of presence, "To be": Eva states that what she longed for was "To be, to become—I had never been." "I was *beginning* to be." According to Eva, Iseult then "sent me back again—to be nothing. . . . I remain gone. Where am I? I do not know—I was cast out from where I believed I was." "Cast out" from the Garden, this Eve yearns only to return, and to reenter the Adamic structure of naming which had originally marked her exclusion.

Iseult's sending of Eva "back," out of language, parallels her own backing away, from the potential inherent in her own language. It is possible that it was Eva's very outlandishness that both attracted and repelled this English teacher. As Eva tries to explain later:

> "Only then, I saw that she hated me, hated the work she had feared to finish. And I who WAS that work, who had hoped so much—how should I not hate her? She saw. Twice over. She could not abide me there; I became a witness. How she had cast away everything, she had seen me see."

What is it about this "work" that Iseult fears so deeply? Her fear may be measured by her retreat: she "had cast away everything" for her entrance into marriage. Her marriage, in fact, cancels her creativity: she does only translations now. A fear of her powers of authorship seems to haunt her, not only because of the betrayal of her own self which authoring would involve, but precisely because of what she *might* author, given the chance. Eva is already half-monstrous, a "giantess." What would she wreak upon the world if she were given the tools of language, and if she were put into writing? And what new language might she come up with? Already Eva suggests a form of language which would disrupt all the old forms, and a form of story which would resist not only sequence and causality, but the ordinary conventions of probability.

Yet, as with Louie or Portia, such possibilities for a new language remain utopian and unrealized, and meanwhile no resolution between "tongues" can be found. Eva attempts first to retreat into the mother-tongue by becoming a mother herself, and authoring a silent text: with the deaf-mute Jeremy, whose origins are wholly unknown, Eva forms a "cinematographic existence, with no soundtrack"; they are "cocooned," "near as twins in the womb." Yet, largely through the agency of other characters, Eva begins to abandon this world and to enter, finally, the other, that of the dominant discourse, which is allied with her plans to marry. In an exaggerated version of Eva's own feelings of abandonment by Iseult, when Iseult left her to go "back" into silence, Jeremy experiences abandonment by Eva, as she leaves him in his silence and pushes on into the language of convention. Yet Eva never enters the train, or the marriage, which become metaphors for her acquisition of the connections and bonds language brings her into, for Jeremy murders her in the last few sentences of the novel. It is, this time, the silent self who kills the self in language; the schizophrenia is now complete. No third term remains.

Eva Trout, as Elizabeth Bowen's last fully imagined character, achieves such haunting magnitude because she embodies all that resides in a femaleness which asks to be expressed, but which can find no expression. From the perspective of those inside the language and stories that already exist, this presence appears monstrous because of its capacity to disrupt. It must be defined and bound into some narrative. Yet from the perspective of those outside, it is precisely this language which constitutes betrayal. The double perspective is retained, because it is the doubleness which is problematic. Bowen offers hints of a collapse of this barrier, but her own ambivalence toward such collapse prevents her from allowing it narrative representation, and the possibility for such representation, in any case, remains questionable. She leaves us always, however, with the desire to imagine a language and a narrative form, however utopian, that would overcome the treacherous distance she herself presents between author and object, and between those women who possess language and those who do not.

CLARE HANSON

The Free Story

Writing of the short story and the cinema, both "young" arts in which she found intriguing similarities, Elizabeth Bowen suggested in 1937 that

> The new literature, whether written or visual, is an affair of reflexes, of immediate susceptibility, of associations not examined by reason: it does not attempt a synthesis. Narrative of any length involves continuity, sometimes a forced continuity: it is here that the novel too often becomes invalid.

In the same essay she coined the term "free story," and defined that freedom in terms of lack of a sponsoring tradition. For her the free story was utterly divorced from folk narrative tradition: it was, literally, a new art, the "child of this century." It is not clear whether she made any distinction between the free story and modernist short fiction: the reference to the "lack of a sponsoring tradition" suggests that the two new forms merged in her mind. Indeed, it appears that the free story has not yet been adequately distinguished from modernist short fiction, though the two types can be clearly separated in chronological and formal terms.

The free story must be treated as a separate entity, distinct from modernist short fiction, because although it too comes under the broad category of short fiction rather than short story (I retain the term "free story" for purely historical reasons), it is in experimental terms a retrogressive form. The free story does not go beyond, but rather turns its back on, many of the

From *Short Stories and Short Fictions, 1880–1980*. © 1985 by Clare Hanson. Macmillan, 1985.

barriers broken by the modernists. Perhaps the question of characterisation is the most important here. Symbolist and modernist short fiction had interrogated the concept of a coherent, historical character, whereas the free story may often pivot on the exploration of character in the traditional sense. Characters are seen as internally coherent and consistent in time: human beings are valued for their "character" in the sense of their uniqueness and idiosyncrasy.

Such a concern for the contingent and specific extends into other areas of the free story. Character and locale, for example, are usually closely delineated by free story writers, who are attracted to the particular rather than the general. They rarely use description for symbolic purposes: the emphasis is on the particular, concrete subject. So V. S. Pritchett writes that the short story is for him: "a form which depends on intensifying the subject, stamping a climate on it, getting the essence of it." The free story also shows far more response to social pressures than does modernist short fiction. This shift in emphasis may be ascribed in part to the impact of the Second World War, which affected civilian life as the First World War did not. It is significant that immediately after the war, when Elizabeth Bowen, V. S. Pritchett and Graham Greene joined in a debate on the question "Why Do I Write?," their major preoccupation was with the writer's relationship to society. All three writers affirmed the importance of this relationship, in an unequivocal manner which would have startled their modernist precursors.

Such aspects of the free story would suggest that it has closer affinities with the novel than with, say, a lyric poem. The interest in social issues, in particular, seems to link the free story with the novel form, and this may account for the number of novelists who, when writing in the short form, have turned to the free story. Angus Wilson and Joyce Cary are examples. Yet these novelists are rarely completely successful in this, and for the free story as for other short story and fiction forms, it remains true that there are only certain writers who, in Elizabeth Bowen's words, "show in this form a special, unique release of their faculties," and who, by their gifts, give the form "new direction and force." Such writers are almost invariably writers in the short form before they are novelists: this is true of V. S. Pritchett and William Sansom and, I suggest, of Bowen herself. As her first biographer has indicated, in the "judgment of posterity" it seems likely that her short fiction will be valued above her novels.

The free story comes into the category of short fiction rather than short story because, despite the name Elizabeth Bowen gave it, it is not primarily biased towards narrative. Plot, in so far as it exists, is there to reveal character—the art of the free story writer is, in Pritchett's words, to catch people at the moment when, through action or speech, "the inner life exposes itself unguardedly." Plot is not there, as it often is in the short story proper, for didactic purposes, nor is it there to express through its own structure a metaphysical truth. Like modernist short fiction, the free story is thus typically inconclusive as narrative. Elizabeth Bowen has written:

> The art of the short story permits a break at what in the novel would be the crux of the plot: the short story, free from the *longueurs* of the novel is also exempt from the novel's conclusiveness—too often forced and false: it may thus more nearly than the novel approach aesthetic and moral truth.

The contention that "aesthetic and moral truth" are by definition shifting and relative links the free story with Impressionist painting. Scene and vision are still more important in the free story than in modernist short fiction, and it is not coincidence that the principal writers considered in this chapter [of *Short Stories and Short Fictions*] all wished initially to paint rather than to write. Elizabeth Bowen studied painting for a short while before turning to short fiction; V. S. Pritchett has described his early passion for that most evanescent medium, watercolour; and William Sansom has described himself as a "painter *manqué*." The analogy between the free story and Impressionism can be pressed quite far. Like the Impressionists, the free story writers were commited to sensation and perception, and their work is marked by a heightened sensitivity to colour, light and atmosphere. Light takes on an almost mystical significance, the recurrent image of light moving on water suggesting the evanescent nature of human perception and experience. Using a similar image, V. S. Pritchett described the art of Chekhov: "He is asserting that life is a fish that cannot be netted by mood or doctrine, but continually glides away between sun and shadow."

The shifting, interpenetrating relations between subject and object are a central concern of free story writers, though it must be emphasized that in this Impressionist form both subject and object have a status and coherence denied them by modernist and post-modernist writers. Thus there is no great apprehension of, or desire for, the merging of subject and object: interrelation and interaction between the two create the magnetic field in which the free story flourishes. Here Elizabeth Bowen presents a typically tense encounter between subject and object:

> She was house-proud, and led this new friend with a touch of emotion up the path to the porch, across the ambitious raw garden. Davina, however, looked neither to right nor left: in-

doors, she did give one glance of surprise rather than pleasure
round the Harvey living-room, artfully pale and bare, where
through steel-framed windows blue-pink afternoon light flooded
the walls and waxy expanse of floor. . . . Ranged round the cold
brick hearth, three low chairs with sailcloth cushions invited a
confidence everything else forbade.

Such an encounter produces a relationship between subject and object from
which we can extrapolate a vision of society: the encounter is not intended
to create a mood in the Symbolist or modernist sense.

A further analogy which might be pursued is that between the free story
and film. Elizabeth Bowen described techniques which she felt had been
taken over from the cinema: "oblique narration, cutting, the unlikely placing of emphasis." Verbal equivalents of these techniques are used in the free
story, and metonymic cutting devices, in particular, enable the free story
writers to combine the brevity prescribed by the early modernists with a
wider range of social reference.

The free story writers' interest in character has been emphasised, and in
fact Freudian theory provides much of the underpinning for their work.
Freud's writings were not widely known in England until the twenties and
thirties, and it was then, rather than in the early modernist period, that his
influence was most widely felt in literature. The Freudian model of the
superego, ego and id did not seem, initially, to conflict with the notion of a
relatively fixed identity; whereas the diagnostic aspects of his work, and in
particular the idea that the unconscious self could be revealed through such
mechanisms as the lapsus, the dream and the joke, had particular relevance
for short fiction writers. Elizabeth Bowen elaborates:

Man has to live how he can: overlooked and dwarfed he makes
himself his own theatre. Is the drama inside heroic or pathologi-
cal? Outward acts have often an inside magnitude. The short
story, with its shorter span than the novel's, with its freedom
from forced complexity, its possible lucidity, is able, like the
poetic drama, to measure man by his aspirations and dreams and
place him alone on that stage which, inwardly, every man is
conscious of occupying alone.

V. S. Pritchett also stresses the idea of "revelation" when he writes that his
characters "live for projecting the fantasies of their inner, imaginative life
and the energies that keep them going."

Revelation, vision—such terms point forward to a Surrealist quality which we will find in the free story of the war years. Another analogy with visual art—but the free story is itself so slippery of definition that often the best means of conveying a quality or aspect of the form is by such analogy. Perhaps Elizabeth Bowen has best summed up the qualities of the form—though not without recourse to metaphor:

> This century's emotion . . . makes a half-conscious artist of every feeling man. Peaks of common experience soar past an altitude-line into poetry. There is also a level immediately below this, on which life is being more and more constantly lived, at which emotion crystallises without going icy, from which a fairly wide view is at command. This level the short story is likely to make its own.

If in this context we substitute "free story" for short story, and equate the poetic "peaks of emotion" with the epiphany of modernist short fiction, we may have a fairly clear picture of the place, range and scope of the free story.

The "discrepancy between fact or circumstance and feeling and the romantic will," a phrase used by Elizabeth Bowen in an essay in *Collected Impressions* (1950), identifies the central conflict in her short fiction, as in her novels. Usually this conflict is focused through the juxtaposition of the romantic consciousness of an adolescent and the jaded awareness of the adults who surround him or her. The world of adulthood, of "maturity," is presented as almost uniformly diminished and disappointing. In Elizabeth Bowen's fiction the adult finds it impossible to recover the grand forms and dreams of childhood. A character in the story "The Disinherited" thus articulates a common perception: "One is empowered to live fully: occasion does not offer." The theme of disillusion—a form of revelation—is clearly well suited to the short fiction form, and need not be seen in wholly negative terms. As Elizabeth Bowen writes:

> Even stories which end in the air, which are comments on or pointers to futility, imply that men and women are too big or too good for the futility in which they are involved. Even to objectify futility is something.

The process of attrition which she sees in the maturing of the individual is mirrored for her on a wider historical scale. Modern life is presented as characteristically "dwarfed," and the architectural imagery which appears frequently in her fiction develops our sense of a change in scale, a loss of the grand style in a modern world. "Over-looked and dwarfed" man can find his theatre, his appropriate setting, in imagination only.

"Ann Lee's" is the title story of a collection published as early as 1926. It is interesting because it is a story "about" a character in a sense that would not be possible in modernist short fiction. Ann Lee is viewed externally, and revealed, in as much as she is revealed, through her actions and speech, which are located in a particular social setting. Her social and professional status is delineated very precisely: she runs a hat shop in the "miserable back streets" which lie behind Sloane Square, yet she is vulgarly described by one of her clientele as "practically a lady," and another speaks of her as "not the sort of person, somehow, that one could ask to reduce her things." Ann Lee is first seen framed in a doorway, and the painterly images of the door and mirror run through the story, so that characters are often found or "frozen" in revealing attitudes. Appearance speaks for the characters, just as does environment. Elizabeth Bowen frequently uses a character's setting metonymically: environment is seen as an attribute of personality, effect rather than cause of being. So the exterior of Ann Lee's shop suggests a particular charm:

> Grey-painted woodwork framed a window over which her legend was inscribed in far-apart black letters: "ANN LEE—HATS." In the window there were always just two hats; one on a stand, one lying on a cushion; and a black curtain with a violet border hung behind to make a background for the hats. In the two upper storeys, perhaps, Ann Lee lived mysteriously, but this no known customer had ever inquired, and the black gauze curtains were impenetrable from without.

Ann Lee holds out the promise of romance to the two idle young women who have come to her shop. Themselves graceless and inept, they feel that in possessing one of Ann Lee's hats they will partake of some of her mystery and charm. Social divisions are overturned as these society women are placed in the position of supplicants, their eager manner contrasting with Ann Lee's serenity:

> These were the hats one dreamed about—no, even in a dream one had never directly beheld them; they glimmered rather on the margin of one's dreams. With trembling hands she reached out in Ann Lee's direction to receive them. Ann Lee smiled deprecatingly upon her and them, then went away to fetch some more.

Up to this point the story has been concerned with certain codes of behaviour, which have been questioned through the simple juxtaposition of Ann Lee, whose poverty "sets off" her economic and aesthetic independence, and the two clients, consumers who devote their life to the spending of the money of others. The level of the story is deepened through the introduction of a subplot. Just before the two women leave the shop a stranger comes in, letting in a sudden draught of cold air. He is instantly recognised as a type by one of the women, Miss Ames:

> As a matter of fact she was recognising him; not as his particular self but as an Incident. He—It—crops up periodically in the path of any young woman who has had a bit of a career.

This "recognition" tells us something about both Miss Ames and Ann Lee: now Ann Lee seems to lose some of her Madonna-like quality. However, the oblique, glancing conclusion of the fiction gives us more insight into the implacability of character which protects her despite her ambiguous social position. As the visitors make their way back to Sloane Square, the stranger stumbles past them in the fog, sobbing. Ann Lee has certainly been firm:

> A square man, sunk deep into an overcoat, scudded across their patch of visibility. By putting out a hand they could have touched him. He went by them blindly; his breath sobbed and panted. It was by his breath that they knew how terrible it had been— terrible.
>
> Passing them quite blindly, he stabbed his way on into the fog.

"Ann Lee's," despite its brevity, deals with Jamesian themes; in particular with the complex relations between money, morality and taste. Its structure is loose and episodic: there is an almost conscious asymmetry in the fiction with its rushed subplot, which reminds us of Elizabeth Bowen's note on the "unlikely placing of emphasis" in new fiction.

"The Little Girl's Room" (1934) could also be traced back to James, with its emphasis on the violence which may lurk in the mind of even the most docile of young girls. It may be useful to compare this fiction with Katherine Mansfield's "The Doll's House," in order to illustrate more clearly the differences between the modernist and the "free" forms of short fiction.

In reading "The Little Girl's Room" our first response is to the author's delicate handling of social nuance. We are taken into a very specific, and very English, social setting, which cannot be adequately characterised by the use of a simple label such as middle-middle class. The little girl of the title lives with her step-grandmother in a house of muffled and oppressive luxury. The décor establishes the tone of a household in which opulence is at war with good taste:

So the child came to Mrs Letherton-Channing's house, where one
had the impression of dignified exile, where British integrity
seemed to have camped on a Tuscan hill, where English mid-
summer did not exceed Italian April—roses wearing into July an
air of delicate pre-maturity—and high noon reflected upon the
ceilings a sheen of ilex and olive. Here the very guests seemed
expatriate, and coal-fires, ruddy ghosts of themselves, roared
under mantles crusted and swagged with glazed Della Robbia
lemons and bluish pears. Clara Ellis, who was at least sincerely
malicious, professed to adore this little Italy from Wigmore Street.

Likewise, respectability clashes with vulgarity. As Geraldine enters a room
we are told that: "At first Clara Ellis frowned: talk of a first-rate scandalous
quality had been held up."

Against this background Geraldine stands out clearly, a neglected child
who has become passively selfish and malicious by default. Her isolation
from other children, added to the fact that every initiative of hers is immediately overtaken by her grandmother (as the author puts it, "Each young
tendril put out found a wire waiting"), has made it impossible for her to
develop her character through the normal channels of expression. Only in
her daydreams can repressed fears and desires find some kind of outlet:

She asked, "General Littlecote,": they replied: "*He is massacred
too.*" She saw his foolish old face lie in blood on a staircase, and
spread out her hand to her side, in terror, close to her thumping
heart. Her cheeks blazed. The rope of excitement she had been
playing out guardedly, sparingly, now fled through her fingers,
burning. She began to shout "*I defy—!*" and stamped on the
mild carpet.

The narrative line of "The Little Girl's Room" could be said to be
marred by the inclusion in the fiction of some adventitious material, particularly in the light of Bowen's own indictment of work in which "some adventitious emotion starts to deform the story." Yet her fiction progresses adven-
titiously, and in this differs sharply from modernist short fiction, which is
deliberately shaped round a central symbolic intention. Her writing progresses to a considerable extent by means of casual association, and it is
thanks to this process that we are given in "The Little Girl's Room" such
delights as Miss Weekes, the "resident lady gardener":

[She] remained in outlook resolutely Old English. She whistled;
the smock and breeches in which she worked were an offence to

Mrs Letherton-Channing, who had engaged her to look after the frames and hot-houses, not expecting her to emerge from these. She had discovered that Miss Weekes morris-danced, that she did rush-work, that she participated in every possible movement to build Jerusalem in this pleasant and green part of Berkshire.

What haunts us, finally, about this particular short fiction is the atmosphere produced by the interaction of a particular character and her environment. In Geraldine, Elizabeth Bowen is concerned with a specific, a special, case, and it is the flavour of the contingent and specific which marks the story. There is no suggestion that the central figure is to be considered symbolic in a wider sense.

Katherine Mansfield's "The Doll's House" is, like "The Little Girl's Room," centred in the consciousness of a young girl sensing for the first time some of the pressures of adult life. "The Doll's House" is set in New Zealand, but many have read it without realising that the setting is not English, for in Katherine Mansfield's fiction there is no place for the kind of exact social reference and placing of atmosphere which is so important in that of Bowen. The external setting of "The Doll's House" is unimportant and is characterised only by a few brief phrases. We learn much more about the miniature doll's house than about its "real" setting within the story, for the doll's house functions as a major image, figuring the bourgeois family home from which the little girl Kezia is emerging, which she is slowly preparing to indict, even perhaps to destroy. The material comfort and prosperity of bourgeois life is highlighted through the description of the doll's house:

> All the walls were papered. There were pictures on the walls, painted on the paper, with gold frames complete. Red carpet covered all the floors except the kitchen; red plush chairs in the drawing-room, green in the dining room; tables, beds with real bedclothes, a cradle, a stove.

Additionally, images of the circle and square run through the story, re-enforcing the idea of the "line which had to be drawn somewhere," to quote Kezia's mother, between the haves and the have-nots. The focal image of "The Doll's House," however, is that of the lamp, which figures grace, or an illumination beyond one's own petty desires. There is also of course a biblical reference to "the light of the world."

What remains with us from "The Doll's House" is a final, emblematic image. Two outcast children sit on a grass verge, expelled from the backyard of Kezia's home. However one of them, at least, has felt with Kezia the promise held out by the lamp:

> Presently our Else nudged up close to her sister. But now she had forgotten the cross lady. She put out a finger and stroked her sister's quill; she smiled her rare smile.
> "I seen the little lamp," she said softly.
> Then both were silent once more.

It could be argued that the "long short" fiction is the form in which Elizabeth Bowen found a "unique release" of her talents and faculties. In this type of fiction a number of characters may drift against each other, revealing personality and feeling only to an extent (we remember that Elizabeth Bowen's first book of stories had the tentative title *Encounters*); they may also be grouped together according to no apparent pattern or order. This sense of a lack of order and cohesion in modern life was something which she was particularly anxious to convey, and which she associated very largely with the dislocations caused by the Second World War.

In "Summer Night" (1941), form and content are as one: the author's sense of the shifting and unsatisfactory nature of human contact is mirrored in the dislocations of the narrative. As one of the characters in the fiction aptly remarks:

> I was saying we should have to find a new form. . . . A new form for thinking and feeling. . . .
> I say, this war's an awful illumination; it's destroyed our dark; we have to see where we are. Immobilised, God help us, and each so far apart that we can't even try to signal each other.

One of the most striking aspects of "Summer Night" is the author's handling in it of cinematic and metonymic cutting devices. Bowen moves in an abrupt and apparently casual fashion among the lives of her characters, who are often linked simply by a contiguity of setting or time of day. So an estranged husband and wife share little but the "lovely night" which just sustains their conventional conversation on the telephone. Ironically, the only person who feels that she can communicate with others is deaf, and her deafness, rather than giving her an intuitive understanding of others, merely protects her from the knowledge of failure in communication.

Characterisation is unusually open-ended in "Summer Night." In the case of each character we are left with a sense of the possibility of change, of a gathering together of latent forces. Meanwhile we, like the other characters, learn more about other people from their environment than from their action or speech. Elizabeth Bowen's extraordinary talent for the creation of atmosphere is most effectively released for this purpose. The description of Aunt Fran's room quoted below is an example. Aunt Fran is the elderly, unmarried sister of the pompous "Major" whose wife has left him to spend the night with another man. The marginal nature of Aunt Fran's existence in his house is beautifully intimated:

> Round the room, on ledges and brackets, stood the fetishes she travelled through life with. They were mementoes—photos in little warped frames, musty, round straw boxes, china kittens, palm crosses, the three Japanese monkeys, *bambini*, a Lincoln Imp, a merry-thought pen-wiper, an ivory spinning-wheel from Cologne. From these objects the original virtue had by now almost evaporated. These gifts' givers, known on her lonely journey, were by now faint as their photogaphs: she no longer knew, now, where anyone was. All the more, her nature clung to these objects that moved with her slowly towards the dark.
>
> Her room, the room of a person tolerated, by now gave off the familiar scent of her self—the smell of the old. A little book wedged the mirror at the angle she liked. When she was into her ripplecloth dressing-gown she brushed and plaited her hair and took out her teeth.

"Summer Night" is concerned with the interlocking rather than with the meeting of lives, yet it is remarkable for the intimate sense of life which it conveys, a sense of vibrations caught and then missed in the steady air. A majestic landscape presides over all:

> As the sun set its light slowly melted the landscape, till everything was made of fire and glass. Released from the glare of noon, the haycocks now seemed to float on the aftergrass: their freshness penetrated the air. In the not far distance hills with woods up their flanks lay in light like hills in another world—it would be a pleasure of heaven to stand up there, where no foot ever seemed to have trodden, on the spaces between the woods soft as powder dusted over with gold.

"Mysterious Kôr" is more directly concerned than "Summer Night" with the effects of the war. The title comes from a poem written in another age, when, as one of the characters puts it: "they thought they had got everything taped, because the whole world had been explored, even the middle of Africa." The two protagonists, Pepita and Arthur, feel the effects of the war in their personal life. They have been separated for a long while, and on Arthur's short leave can find nowhere to go where they can be alone. They loiter outside the gates of Regent's Park, reluctant to return to the flat which Pepita shares with the well-meaning but dense Callie who does not realise that on this particular occasion she might be *de trop* in the small flat.

As they stand at the entrance to the park, Pepita and Arthur watch the moon transforming the London cityscape:

> Full moonlight drenched the city and searched it; there was not a niche left to stand in. The effect was remorseless: London looked like the moon's capital—shallow, cratered, extinct. It was late, but not yet midnight; now the buses had stopped the polished roads and streets in this region sent for minutes together a ghostly unbroken reflection up. The soaring new flats and the crouching old shops and houses looked equally brittle under the moon, which blazed in windows that looked its way. The futility of the black-out became laughable: from the sky, presumably, you could see every slate in the roofs, every whited kerb, every contour of the naked winter flowerbeds in the park; and the lake, with its shining twists and tree-darkened islands would be a landmark for miles, yes, miles, overhead.

After they have stood for some minutes, Pepita draws away from Arthur murmuring "Mysterious Kôr." "Mysterious Kôr" is something which Pepita in particular has built out of such dislocated moments as this—it has become an image which speaks to and reveals her subconscious desires. In this sense it is Surrealist, expressing desire through the kind of dislocated images which occur in dreams. For Pepita it is a dehumanised landscape which is desired and imagined. It is as though the ties of love and affection have become too much to bear in the uncertain world of the war: as though she seeks relief even from Arthur. A dream which extends the image of "Mysterious Kôr" closes the story:

> She still lay, as she had lain, in an avid dream, of which Arthur had been the source, of which Arthur was not the end. With him she looked this way, that way, down the wide, void, pure streets, between statues, pillars and shadows, through archways and colonnades. With him she went up the stairs down which nothing but moon came; with him trod the ermine dust of the endless halls, stood on terraces, mounted the extreme tower, looked down on the statued squares, the wide, void, pure streets. He was

the password, but not the answer: it was to Kôr's finality that she turned.

"Mysterious Kôr" works on a high level of emotion through the use of hallucinatory landscapes invested with all the anxiety of dream. It is an "inward" story of the war, concerned with dislocations of private life and with the emotional rather than the physical effects of the war. As Arthur puts it to Callie in a rare moment of confidence:

> It makes me feel cruel the way I unsettle her: I don't know how much it's me myself or how much it's something the matter that I can't help. . . . They forget war's not just only war; it's years out of people's lives that they've never had before and won't have again.

"Mysterious Kôr" is a *tour de force*, catching the atmosphere of the forced conjunction of three people whose nerves have been frayed by the war. It is a short fiction which illustrates almost perfectly what Elizabeth Bowen meant when she wrote that for her "the short story is a matter of vision, rather than of feeling."

ALFRED CORN

An Anglo-Irish Novelist

W hen Quentin Bell's biography of Virginia Woolf appeared in 1975 the Woolf revival already underway picked up momentum. Victoria Glendinning's *Elizabeth Bowen* probably won't do the same for her. For one thing, Bowen's story lacks the best-seller ingredients Woolf's had—Bohemianism, sexual irregularity, madness, suicide. Beyond that, Glendinning's book, a serviceable, journalistic account, is not so acute as Bell's and much less committed; she seems to doubt the value of her subject. Understandably, Bowen could be described as a disciple of Woolf's, and, since disciples tend to be lesser figures than their masters, Bowen may not be as important as Woolf. She died in 1973 and is still in that limbo the recently deceased are consigned to until critics and the public make up their minds about these writers' historical place and artistic worth. Glendinning merely registers the present uncertainty; she doesn't come down solidly in Bowen's favor— implicitly calling into question the need for this biography.

Glendinning doesn't settle the issue, but at least she poses it, and she had a thesis. She sees Bowen's Anglo-Irish background as the source not just of some of her "material" but of her creativity in general; and "life with the lid on" (Bowen's phrase to describe how she learned in childhood to manage with the personal and domestic confusions facing her) as the dampening influence on that creativity. The first part of the thesis is beyond dispute, unless one ignores Bowen's own statements about the question, and the evidence in her fiction. But, precisely, the Anglo-Irish temperament *includes*

From *The Metamorphoses of Metaphor: Essays in Poetry and Fiction.* © 1987 by Viking Penguin, Inc.

the second part. That peculiar temperament emerged as a compound of the local Irish enthusiasm and the imposed English civil and moral order. Installed in large numbers as landowners under the Protectorate, the English stood in roughly the same relationship to the indigenous Catholic population as the superego does to the unconscious mind. But the Irish spirit of place is strong, and succeeding generations were naturally affected by it. Elizabeth Bowen, brought up on lands that had been granted to an ancestor in 1653, came into the conflict as part of her birthright; and it is really intrinsic to her fiction, where all the disturbing forces in psychic life are harnessed to a highly controlled, lucid sense of form. There would hardly be so much control without a need for it; the effect on Bowen's work is not regrettable, but instead beneficent, to judge from those occasional instances where control slips.

If Elizabeth Bowen hadn't left the family seat (an austerely handsome eighteenth-century house named Bowen's Court) she might never have fully developed the English side of her character. Inevitably, she would have been a different writer. She has stated that the Irish don't separate art from artifice, which is arguably better suited to the stage than to the novel— hence Goldsmith, Sheridan, Wilde, Shaw, Beckett, and the others. "Possibly it was England made me a novelist," she says; and for that reason her immigration to England at age seven took on, when she wrote about it in her memoirs much later, a fateful quality.

Elizabeth's father, Henry Bowen, always a "dreamy" man, had a series of nervous collapses beginning when she was six. Finally he had to be committed; whereupon Elizabeth and her mother went to stay with relatives across the Channel. They were passed from hand to hand among several towns along the Kentish coast. Elizabeth seemed unharmed by this, at least on the surface, but she did develop a marked stammer about this time and kept it the rest of her life. In the main, she embraced her new life and its violent tinge of adventurousness with gusto.

Even so, she never lost touch with Ireland and Bowen's Court. It was always there to be visited, one of the few large houses to escape burning during the Troubles. Bowen described these Irish country houses as "something between a *raison d'être* and a predicament," and the phrase did apply in at least her case. For her Ireland was a heartland, and she took up semipermanent residence at Bowen's Court again in the early 1950s. Eventually living expenses and upkeep forced Bowen to sell the house in 1960. She believed it was going to be occupied by the buyer's likable family, but in fact the property had interested him only because of its timber: Bowen's Court was torn down. The conjunction of these facts—home rule, the end of the Anglo-Irish country house and the Anglo-Irish novel—gives Bowen's life a fabular character, one a self-styled "romantic" must have reflected on at length.

The actual discovery of her vocation and molding of her career took place in London, a series of events displaying a retrospective plausibility they cannot have had for the Elizabeth Bowen who arrived there in 1918. A national capital acts as a lodestone to potential artists, conferring its magnetism on those capable of being charged with it. Bowen, detecting in herself the instincts of an artist, and having come to the city where it was possible to be one, at first mistook the medium: she enrolled in the London County Council School of Art and tried to paint. This came to nothing. Perhaps she had assumed her alert eye would naturally bring with it the gift of rendering visual insights on canvas. An error, but in her case not tragic—she discovered that the visible world can be powerfully presented in fiction. By the time Bowen's desire to paint had abandoned her, she'd begun to write stories. She had also met Rose Macaulay, who recommended the stories to an editor. When they were published, Bowen's ambitions shifted base for good.

Her first collection of short stories, *Encounters*, came out in 1923, and in that same year she married Alan Cameron. The marriage, or perhaps only its never being dissolved before Cameron's death, always puzzled Bowen's friends. A fault of Glendinning's biography is that it doesn't shed much light on Bowen's choice of a husband. The information she does give only makes things more mysterious—the water has been stirred but only muddied. For now, all that's known is that Bowen seems to have accepted to marry Cameron, a fairly ordinary educational administrator, because marriage represented certified adulthood to her, and Cameron was the first suitor to propose to her whom she considered at all "possible." To this Glendinning adds that Cameron had been at Oxford and would have seemed an intellectual to the half-formed, haphazardly educated girl Bowen was. She also mentions that Cameron took his young wife in hand as to the matter of clothes, suggesting that she dispense with some of the unusual jewelry and directing her toward dresses with straight hems and better cuts. This early phase has its comic probability; but why Bowen didn't, after she became one of the most grown-up women of her time, bid farewell to a man for whom she never felt any passion, who found her writer friends dull and was found dull by them in turn, is an unsolved mystery.

Less of a surprise is Bowen's beginning to have affairs outside the marriage, with Cameron's knowledge and fatalistic consent. This habit would have been more acceptable than plodding fidelity, at least among the worldly set of friends that gradually devolved on Bowen as she became known as a novelist. (Some of them she met during her years living at Oxford; others belong to the period of her return to London and taking up residence in a pretty house in Regent's Park.) Even though one or two of the young men she favored seem to have been odd choices, they must have struck friends such as C. M. Bowra and Cyril Connolly as commendable alternatives to the eternal husband. The deepest, most lasting, and probably least objectionable to Bowen's friends was the love affair with Charles Ritchie. He was a Canadian diplomat who came to London just before the war and made himself liked by some of the people Bowen spent time with. In his published diary, *The Siren Years,* Ritchie says, "The first time I saw Elizabeth Bowen I thought she looked more like a bridge-player than a poet," apparently not realizing the categories sometimes overlap. Later, he was to note down after one of Bowen's visits, "I owe her everything." The relationship went on full force all through the war and continued many years afterwards, with some long interruptions, despite Ritchie's marriage in 1948. He was attracted by the family ideal and may also have wanted to establish some sort of logistic symmetry with Bowen's own marriage. For her, divorce never seems to have been a real option. Much about Bowen's relationship with Ritchie will remain conjectural until a more complete biography appears.

Another relationship stinted in this book is Bowen's friendship with Virginia Woolf, whom she met in the early 1930s and saw frequently until Woolf's death in 1941. The friendship was formed and held fast in the face of several dividing factors—generational difference, manner of living, artistic goals. It was bound to be complex, and an understanding of it would almost certainly shed light on the work of both women, since there is an influence relationship between them, possibly even a reciprocal one. The critical problems raised are difficult, and it may be this that caused Glendinning to shy away from a full discussion of Bowen and Woolf. But even aside from the relationship, this biography fails to treat Bowen as a writer, to add to our understanding of her achievement. Since her artistic reputation is still in the balance, no opportunity to discuss her worth should be wasted.

At its peak after the publication of *The Heat of the Day* in 1948, Bowen's reputation began to dim not long after. The angry young men of the 1950s could hardly be expected to care for the work of an implacably good-humored older woman who wrote mostly about the comfortably off and with no more satirical edge than the sort any good novelist always has readily at hand. She was associated with Connolly and the *Horizon* circle; even Connolly at last was forced to acknowledge that it was "closing time in the gardens of the West." The new order looked very much like disorder. Novelists committed to innovation accepted Robbe-Grillet's decree that the nineteenth-century bourgeois novel was dead letter and stopped regarding works of classic fiction like *The House in Paris* or *The Death of the Heart* as models. Bowen herself seems to have noticed a shift in the wind and to have responded to it: her last novel, *Eva Trout,* is very different from the earlier ones. Those who are lukewarm about Bowen in general tend to prefer it to the others, and convinced Bowenites like it least. This novel can be praised for having captured some of the harum-scarum quality of life in the jet age; but that comes at a considerable sacrifice of the formal lucidity and sustaining moral vision Bowen was best known for.

As a writer, Bowen must be evaluated on the basis of about a dozen stories and five novels—*The Last September, To the North, The House in Paris, The Death of the Heart,* and *The Heat of the Day.* (A case could be made, too, for *The Little Girls.*) Her nonfiction and autobiographical writings, though they have wit and sometimes genius to recommend them, aren't under consideration here. On the basis of her fiction alone, Bowen is as good as Evelyn Waugh, better than Ivy Compton-Burnett, Graham Greene, or Henry Green. Her novels yield to Woolf's in visionary intensity but are superior to them in formal construction, variety of subject, and moral force.

Bowen is below the greatest novelists—Flaubert, George Eliot, Tolstoy, James, Proust—but like them she reflected constantly and profoundly on the nature of fiction. So much so, that the "laws" of fiction came to constitute a metaphorial system for her, used in the novels themselves sometimes to help present the action, as in this passage from *The Heat of the Day*:

> His concentration on her was made more oppressive by his failure to have or let her give him any possible place in the human scene. By the rules of fiction, with which life to be credible must comply, he was as a character "impossible"—each time they met, for instance, he showed no shred or trace of having been continuous since they last met.

Conversely, Bowen's brilliant "Notes on Writing a Novel" has a poetic, almost an allegorical quality. She can say, for example, "Characters must *materialize*—i.e., must have a palpable, physical reality. . . . Physical personality belongs to action. . . . Eyes, hands, stature, etc., must appear, and only appear, *in play.*" Discussing dialogue, she says, "Speech is what the characters *do to each other.*" And, in general, "The presence, and action of the poetic truth is the motive (or motor) morality of the novel."

It would be wrong, however, to regard Bowen as a rulebook novelist.

The rule she most often waives is the one proscribing authorial comment. Rather like one of the "innocents" in her own novels, Bowen can't keep quiet about what she sees and knows. The proportion of comment to narrative is much higher than Flaubert, say, would have tolerated. Yet Proust commented even more freely than Bowen, and her rushes of insight are often as good as his. In both cases you feel that some principle of genius is at work, so that the propensity must be indulged, and the rules broken—all the more since the results are so startling. As much by their weaknesses as by their strengths do artists come into their own.

Part of the moral energy of Bowen's novels resides in just these passages of authorial comment. In them, she renews for English fiction the tradition of the French *moralistes*—La Rochefoucauld, La Bruyère, and the great women diarists and letter-writers of the eighteenth century. But she is still squarely within the precincts of fiction: these passages arise directly from the action presented, and they illuminate what comes after them. Moreover, Bowen isn't deficient in the way many moralists are, so intent on the meaning, purely, of human action they lack sensory awareness. Bowen is all perception. Reading her you realize you have never paid close enough attention to places or persons, the mosaic of detail that composes the first, or the voices and gestures that reveal the second. Her novels invariably take the point of view of an omniscient narrator; and, if *omniscient* means all-seeing as well as all-knowing, the term is especially apt for Bowen. Of course, this very knowingness can be a fault: the reader may feel as though Bowen is always too far ahead, running circles around reader consciousness. This is an unpleasant sensation if only because it gives, inevitably, an impression of unreality: no one feels that life is told by an omniscient narrator; and that point of view in novels is most effective when least obtrusive. For the most part, however, Bowen strikes the right balance between the transparence and opaqueness of reality.

As a prose stylist Bowen is elegant—but quirky. She casts for the short sentence, the clipped epigram. We don't normally associate delicacy of observation with a percussive syntax like Bowen's, but that is her compound. Reading her is like being pelted with feathers, occasionally the quill end. Critics have sometimes complained about her inversions. Habitually she puts the most important word of a sentence in attack position at the beginning or tonic position at the end. By turns, the sentences can seem mannered or forceful. Certainly they contribute to the Anglo-Irish flavor of her writing. Sentences like hers can only be written by someone who has grown up with a special speech-music in the ear.

R. P. Blackmur notes that in Henry James's last novels there was always "a plot which does truly constitute the soul of the action, which does truly imitate the conditions and aspirations of human like as seen in the actions of men and women of more than usual worth and risk." Bowen would certainly have acknowledged these ideals as her own; and she realized them well—except for the last phrase, "more than usual worth and risk." Consistently she made it a part of novelistic plausibility not to invent larger-than-life characters. The figure, so common in her novels, of the innocent young girl forging toward experience leaves an impression less of "worth and risk" than of the destructiveness of innocence, to self and others. Other kinds of characters in Bowen tend to be all too human; we always look a little down at them. Yet if we are in fact experiencing an "ironic" phase in literature, as understood by Northrop Frye, in which fictional characters are typically marginal, hindered, or "low," Bowen can't be called to special account—she is only doing as other moderns do. Larger-than-life characters in modern fiction? There are none; but their absence is felt more keenly in Bowen's novels because in all other ways they exhibit the characteristic strengths of the nineteenth-century classics. The brilliant, humane analysis, the patient, even heroic notation of physical detail, remind us of the older books, and, so conditioned, we scan Bowen's pages with an unconscious expectation of finding heroes there. Their failure to appear, then, disappoints. On the other hand, Bowen has created many magnetic and memorable characters—Stella in *The Heat of the Day,* Emmeline in *To the North,* and (perhaps the nearest Bowen came to inventing an heroic character) the housemaid Matchett in *The Death of the Heart.* All of these go readily into that stock everyone keeps of fictional persons—characters that have caught special human qualities or attitudes toward experience and come to stand for them. In a fictional world made actual and palpable, Bowen's characters move and make their discoveries, comic or tragic or both together. These novels themselves will soon be rediscovered; new biographical and critical studies would help clarify Bowen's place among English novelists. Weighing real issues, and with a small readjustment of the sights, readers ought to reach a fair view of Elizabeth Bowen—as one of the masters of modern fiction.

Chronology

<table>
<tr><td>1899</td><td>Elizabeth Bowen, only child of Henry Bowen, a barrister, and Florence Colley Bowen, born in Dublin.</td></tr>
<tr><td>1906</td><td>Father suffers mental illness, "brain fever." Bowen and mother move to Kent, where they have relatives.</td></tr>
<tr><td>1912</td><td>Mother dies; Bowen stays with relatives and is sent to the Downe House School in Westerham, Kent.</td></tr>
<tr><td>1916</td><td>Graduates from Downe House School. Returns to Dublin for the duration of World War I, where she works in a hospital for shell-shocked veterans.</td></tr>
<tr><td>1918</td><td>Studies at the London Council School of Art. Quits and travels on the Continent.</td></tr>
<tr><td>1919</td><td>Begins writing stories.</td></tr>
<tr><td>1923</td><td>Encounters, her first collection of stories, published. Quietly marries Alan Charles Cameron; moves to Old Headington, outside Oxford, where Cameron works for the school system. They move in university circles.</td></tr>
<tr><td>1927</td><td>The Hotel published.</td></tr>
<tr><td>1928</td><td>Father dies. Bowen inherits Bowen's Court in County Cork; first woman to own it since its completion in 1776.</td></tr>
<tr><td>1929</td><td>Joining Charles, and Other Stories and The Last September published.</td></tr>
<tr><td>1931</td><td>Friends and Relations.</td></tr>
<tr><td>1932</td><td>To the North.</td></tr>
</table>

1934   *The Cat Jumps, and Other Stories.*

1935   *The House in Paris.* Moves with husband to London, where she lives until 1952. Writes for *The New Statesman.* Friendship with members of the Bloomsbury group, in particular Virginia Woolf.

1938   *The Death of the Heart.*

1941   *Look at All Those Roses: Short Stories.* By this time writes for the Ministry of Information and serves as an air raid warden. She and her husband remain in London during the Blitz.

1942   *Bowen's Court,* recounting the history of the house. *Seven Winters,* reminiscences of childhood.

1945   *The Demon Lover and Other Stories.*

1948   Made a Commander of the British Empire.

1949   *The Heat of the Day.* During the 1940s is the regular book reviewer for *The Tatler.* Awarded honorary Doctor of Letters degree by Trinity College, Dublin.

1950   *Collected Impressions,* essays, reviews, prefaces.

1952   Husband, never fully recovered from wounding in World War I, dies. Bowen moves to Bowen's Court.

1955   *A World of Love.*

1957   Honorary Doctor of Letters, Oxford University. Associate editor of *London Magazine.*

1960   Sells Bowen's Court, moves back to Old Headington.

1962   *Afterthoughts,* pieces about writing.

1964   *The Little Girls.*

1965   *A Day in the Dark.*

1969   *Eva Trout.*

1973   Dies in London.

1975   *Pictures and Conversations,* a collection of essays and articles, published posthumously.

Contributors

HAROLD BLOOM, Sterling Professor of the Humanities at Yale University, is the author of *The Anxiety of Influence, Poetry and Repression,* and many other volumes of literary criticism. A MacArthur Prize Fellow, he is general editor of five series of literary criticism published by Chelsea House.

MONA VAN DUYN has taught at Washington University and was for many years editor of *Perspective.* Her poems, stories, and reviews have appeared in *Sewanee Review, Kenyon Review, Poetry,* and *Transatlantic Review.* She is the author of *Letters from Father and Other Poems* and *Merciful Disguises: Published and Unpublished Poems.*

WILLIAM HEATH is Professor of English at Amherst College, and the author of *Wordsworth and Coleridge* as well as editor of *Major British Poets of the Romantic Period* and *Discussions of Jane Austen.*

EDWARD MITCHELL is Professor of English at Ohio University, the editor of *Henry Miller: Three Decades of Criticism,* and co-editor of *Continental Short Stories: The Modern Tradition.*

RICHARD GILL is Professor of English at Pace University in New York. He is the author of *Happy Rural Seat: The English Country House and the Literary Imagination.*

HARRIET BLODGETT is the author of *Patterns of Reality: Elizabeth Bowen's Novels.*

BARBARA BELLOW WATSON is Professor of English and Director of the Women's Studies Program at City College in New York.

HERMIONE LEE is Lecturer in English and Related Literature at the University of York and the author of *The Novels of Virginia Woolf* and *Philip Roth,* as well as the editor of *Stevie Smith, A Selection.*

HARRIET S. CHESSMAN is Assistant Professor of English at Yale University. She is at work on a book entitled *Women, Writing, and Silence in the Twentieth-Century Novel.*

CLARE HANSON is the author of *Short Stories and Fictions: 1880–1980* and co-author, with Andrew Gurr, of *Katherine Mansfield.*

ALFRED CORN, poet and literary critic, has taught poetry at Columbia, Yale, and other universities. He is the author of four books of poetry: *All Roads at Once, A Call in the Midst of the Crowd, The Various Light,* and *Notes from a Child of Paradise.*

Bibliography

Adams, Timothy Dow. " 'Bend Sinister': Duration in Elizabeth Bowen's *The House in Paris.*" *International Fiction Review* 7, no. 1 (1980): 49–52.

Atkins, John. *Six Novelists Look at Society.* London: John Calder, 1977.

Austin, Allan E. *Elizabeth Bowen.* New York: Twayne, 1971.

Blodgett, Harriet. *Patterns of Reality: Elizabeth Bowen's Novels.* The Hague: Mouton, 1975.

Brooke, Jocelyn. *Elizabeth Bowen.* New York: Longmans, Green, 1952.

Brooke-Rose, Christine. "Lady Precious Stream." *London Magazine* 4, no. 2 (1964): 83–86.

Brothers, Barbara. "Pattern and Void: Bowen's Irish Landscape and *The Heat of the Day.*" *Mosaic* 12, no. 3 (1979): 129–38.

Church, Margaret. "The Irish Writer, Elizabeth Bowen, 'Her Table Spread': Allusion and 'Anti-Roman.' " *Folio* 11 (August 1978): 17–20.

Coles, Robert. *Irony in the Mind's Life: Essays on Novels by James Agee, Elizabeth Bowen, and George Eliot.* Charlottesville: University of Virginia Press, 1974.

Coles, William. "The Pattern of Responsibility in the Novels of Elizabeth Bowen." *Harvard Advocate* 137 (December 1952): 20–22, 37–40.

Daiches, David. "The Novels of Elizabeth Bowen." *English Journal* 38, no. 6 (1949): 305–13.

Davenport, Gary T. "Elizabeth Bowen and the Big House." *Southern Humanities Review* 8 (1974): 27–34.

Dorenkamp, Angela G. " 'Fall or Leap': Bowen's *The Heat of the Day.*" *Critique: Studies in Modern Fiction* 10, no. 3 (1968): 13–21.

Dunleavy, J. E. "The Subtle Satire of Elizabeth Bowen and Mary Lavin." *Tulsa Studies in Women's Literature* 2 (1983): 69–82.

Fraustino, Daniel V. "Elizabeth Bowen's 'The Demon Lover': Psychosis or Seduction?" *Studies in Short Fiction* 17 (1980): 483–87.

Gindin, James. "Ethical Structures in John Galsworthy, Elizabeth Bowen, and Iris Murdoch." In *Forms of Modern British Fiction,* edited by Alan Warren Friedman. Austin: University of Texas Press, 1975.

Glendinning, Victoria. *Elizabeth Bowen: Portrait of a Writer.* New York: Knopf, 1978.

Greene, George. "Elizabeth Bowen: Imagination as Therapy." *Perspective* 14 (1965): 42–52.

Hall, James W. *The Lunatic Giant in the Drawing Room.* Bloomington: Indiana University Press, 1968.

Harkness, Bruce. "The Fiction of Elizabeth Bowen." *English Journal* 44, no. 9 (1955): 499–506.

Hawkins, Desmond. "Fiction Chronicle." *Criterion* 18, no. 70 (1938): 82–92.

Heath, William. *Elizabeth Bowen: An Introduction to Her Novels.* Madison: University of Wisconsin Press, 1961.

Heinemann, Alison. "The Indoor Landscape in Bowen's *The Death of the Heart.*" *Critique: Studies in Modern Fiction* 10, no. 3 (1968): 5–12.

Hughes, Douglass A. "Cracks in the Psyche: Elizabeth Bowen's 'The Demon Lover.'" *Studies in Short Fiction* 10 (1973): 411–13.

Karl, Frederick R. *A Reader's Guide to the Contemporary English Novel.* Rev. ed. New York: Farrar, Straus & Giroux, 1972.

Kenney, Edwin J. *Elizabeth Bowen.* Lewisburg, Pa.: Bucknell University Press, 1974.

Kiely, Benedict. "Elizabeth Bowen." *Irish Monthly* 78 (1950): 175–81.

———. *Modern Irish Fiction: A Critique.* Dublin: Golden Eagle Books, 1950.

Lee, Hermione. *Elizabeth Bowen: An Estimation.* Totowa, N.J.: Barnes & Noble, 1981.

———. "The Placing of Loss: Elizabeth Bowen's *To the North.*" *Essays in Criticism* 28 (1978): 129–42.

Markovič, Vida E. *The Changing Face: Disintegration of Personality in the Twentieth-Century British Novel, 1900–1950.* Carbondale: Southern Illinois University Press, 1970.

McDowell, Alfred. "*The Death of the Heart* and the Human Dilemma." *Modern Language Studies* 8, no. 2 (1978): 5–16.

McGowan, Martha. "The Enclosed Garden in Elizabeth Bowen's *A World of Love.*" *Eire* 16, no. 1 (1981): 55–70.

Medoff, Jeslyn. "There Is No Elsewhere: Elizabeth Bowen's Perceptions of War." *Modern Fiction Studies* 30, no. 1 (1984): 73–81.

Meredith, David W. "Authorial Detachment in Elizabeth Bowen's 'Ann Lee's.'" *Massachusetts Studies in English* 8, no. 2 (1982): 9–20.

O'Faolain, Sean. *The Vanishing Hero: Studies in the Novelists of the Twenties.* London: Eyre & Spottiswoode, 1956.

Parrish, Paul A. "The Loss of Eden: Four Novels of Elizabeth Bowen." *Critique: Studies in Modern Fiction* 15, no. 1 (1973): 86–100.

Pendry, E. D. *The New Feminism of English Fiction: A Study in Contemporary Women Novelists.* Tokyo: Kenyusha, 1956.

Perry, John O. "Elizabeth Bowen and 'The Cat Jumps.'" In *Insight II: Analyses of British Literature,* edited by John V. Hagopian and Martin Dolch. Frankfurt: Hirschgraben, 1965.

Quinn, Antoinette. "Elizabeth Bowen's Irish Stories: 1939 to 1945." In *Studies in Anglo-Irish Literature,* edited by Heinz Kosok. Bonn: Boubier, 1982.

Rule, Jane. *Lesbian Images.* Garden City, N.J.: Doubleday, 1975.

Rupp, Richard H. "The Post-War Fiction of Elizabeth Bowen." *Xavier University Studies* 4, no. 1 (1965): 55–67.

Sackville-West, Edward. "An Appraisal: Ivy Compton-Burnett and Elizabeth Bowen." *Horizon* 13 (June 1946): 367–85.

―――. *Inclinations*. New York: Scribner's, 1949.

Sarton, May. *A World of Light: Portraits and Celebrations*. New York: Norton, 1976.

Saul, George Brandon. "The Short Stories of Elizabeth Bowen." *Arizona Quarterly* 21 (1965): 53–59.

Sellery, J'nan, and William O. Harris. *Elizabeth Bowen: A Bibliography*. Austin: University of Texas Press, 1981.

Seward, Barbara. "Elizabeth Bowen's World of Impoverished Love." *College English* 18, no. 1 (1956): 30–37.

Sharp, Sister M. Corona. "The House as Setting and Symbol in Three Novels by Elizabeth Bowen." *Xavier University Studies* 2, no. 3 (1961): 93–103.

Snow, Lotus. "The Uncertain 'I': A Study of Elizabeth Bowen's Fiction." *Western Humanities Review* 4 (1950): 299–310.

Stokes, Edward. "Elizabeth Bowen: Pre-Assumption or Moral Angle?" *Journal of the Australasian University Language and Literature Association* 11 (September 1959): 35–47.

Strickhausen, H. "Elizabeth Bowen and Reality." *Sewanee Review* 73 (1965): 158–65.

Sullivan, Walter. "A Sense of Place: Elizabeth Bowen and the Landscape of the Heart." *Sewanee Review* 84 (1976): 142–49.

Wagner, Geoffrey. "Elizabeth Bowen and the Artificial Novel." *Essays in Criticism* 13 (1963): 155–63.

Acknowledgments

"Pattern and Pilgrimage: A Reading of *The Death of the Heart*" by Mona Van Duyn from *Critique: Studies in Modern Fiction* 4, no. 2 (Spring/Summer 1961), © 1961 by *Critique*. Reprinted by permission of the Helen Dwight Reid Educational Foundation. Published by Heldref Publications, 4000 Albemarle Street, N.W., Washington, D.C.

"The Jacobean Melodrama of *To The North*" (originally entitled "Manners and Morals") by William Heath from *Elizabeth Bowen: An Introduction to Her Novels* by William Heath, © 1961 by the Regents of the University of Wisconsin. Reprinted by permission of the University of Wisconsin Press.

"Themes in Elizabeth Bowen's Short Stories" by Edward Mitchell from *Critique: Studies in Modern Fiction* 8, no. 3 (Spring/Summer 1966), © 1966 by the Bolingbroke Society, Inc. Reprinted by permission of the Helen Dwight Reid Foundation. Published by Heldref Publications, 4000 Albemarle Street, N.W., Washington, D.C.

"The Country House in a Time of Troubles" (originally entitled "Setting the House in Order: The Country House in a Time of Troubles: Yeats, Bowen, Green, Woolf, Carey, Waugh") by Richard Gill from *Happy Rural Seat: The English Country House and the Literary Imagination* by Richard Gill, © 1972 by Yale University. Reprinted by permission of Yale University Press.

"The Necessary Child: *The House in Paris*" by Harriet Blodgett from *Patterns of Reality: Elizabeth Bowen's Novels* by Harriet Blodgett, © 1975 by Mouton & Co. Reprinted by permission of Mouton de Gruyter, a division of Walter de Gruyter & Co., Berlin, Amsterdam, and New York.

"Variations on an Enigma: Elizabeth Bowen's War Novel" by Barbara Bellow Watson from *Southern Humanities Review* 15, no. 2 (Spring 1981), © 1981 by Auburn University. Reprinted by permission.

"The Bend Back: *A World of Love* (1955), *The Little Girls* (1964), and *Eva Trout* (1968)" by Hermione Lee from *Elizabeth Bowen: An Estimation* by Hermione Lee, © 1981 by Hermione Lee. Reprinted by permission of A. D. Peters & Co. Ltd., Barnes & Noble Books, Totowa, New Jersey, and Vision Press Ltd.

"Women and Language in the Fiction of Elizabeth Bowen" by Harriet S. Chessman from *Twentieth Century Literature* 29, no. 1 (Spring 1983), © 1983 by Hofstra University Press. Reprinted by permission.

"The Free Story" by Clare Hanson from *Short Stories and Short Fictions, 1880–1980* by Clare Hanson, © 1985 by Clare Hanson. Reprinted by permission of the author, Macmillan Press Ltd., and St. Martin's Press, Inc.

"An Anglo-Irish Novelist" (originally entitled "An Anglo-Irish Novelist: Elizabeth Bowen") by Alfred Corn from *The Metamorphoses of Metaphor: Essays in Poetry and Fiction* by Alfred Corn, © 1987 by Viking Penguin, Inc. Reprinted by permission.

Index

"All Saints," 40
"Ann Lee's," 144–45
Anthony Trollope, 103
"Apple Tree, The," 112
Aragon, Louis, 84
Austen, Jane, 88, 100

Beckett, Samuel, 85, 100
Between the Acts (Woolf), 56, 83
"Big House, The," 51
Blackmur, R. P., 158–59
Bowen, Elizabeth Dorothea Cole: Austen compared to, 88, 100; background of, 52, 56, 57, 94, 104–5, 113, 114, 119, 141, 153–56, 157, 158; Beckett compared to, 85, 100; Camus compared to, 100; Cather compared to, 7; class distinctions as viewed by, 95; Compton-Burnett compared to, 157; G. Eliot compared to, 157; T. S. Eliot's influence on, 131; films as viewed by, 139, 142; Flaubert compared to, 157, 158; and Forster, 56, 84, 105, 120; and Freud, 1, 142; Green compared to, 105, 157; Greene compared to, 105, 157; Hartley compared to, 105; innocence as viewed by, 86; James compared to, 1, 3, 4, 7, 51, 157; James's influence on, 1, 52–53, 105, 145; Joyce compared to, 1, 3; Kafka compared to, 100; and Lawrence, 1, 124; Lehmann compared to, 105; Murdoch's influence on, 105; Pater's influence on, 3, 4, 7; Pirandello compared to, 82, 97, 100; and Proust, 112, 115–16, 157, 158; Sartre compared to, 14; Shaw's influence on, 86; short stories as viewed by, 139, 142, 143; Somerville and Ross compared to, 109; Spark's influence on, 105; Tolstoy compared to 157; war as viewed by, 56, 81; Waugh compared to, 51, 56, 157; and Woolf, 84, 105, 124, 153, 156, 157; as writer, 140, 141–42, 143–47, 148–51; Yeats compared to, 51
Bowen, Elizabeth Dorothea Cole, works of: alienation as theme in, 46, 50; class distinctions as theme in, 105; external vs. internal reality as theme in, 39, 42; female charac-

ters in, 124–38; hallucination and illusion as theme in, 43–44, 45, 86; the home's importance in, 51–61, 91–92, 97, 100, 143; human community as theme in, 56; innocence vs. experience as theme in, 39–40, 41, 50, 82, 85, 143, 159; isolation as theme in, 56; language vs. silence as theme in, 100–101, 125, 128, 132, 134; psychological insights in, 1–2, 105; reputation of, 156; style of, 1, 158; tradition as theme in, 51; war as theme in, 82, 148. *See also specific works*
Bowen, Henry (father), 154
Bowen's Court: the home's importance in, 51–52; human community as theme in, 58; isolation as theme in, 52; tradition as theme in, 11, 51–52, 56
Bowra, C. M., 156
Brideshead Revisited (Waugh), 56, 83
"Burnt Norton" (Eliot), 131

Cameron, Alan, 104, 113, 155
Camus, Albert, 100
Cary, Joyce, 140
Cather, Willa, 7
Caught (Green), 83
Changing Face, The (Markovič), 86–87
Chekhov, Anton, 141
Collins, Wilkie, 53
Compton-Burnett, Ivy, 157
Connolly, Cyril, 156–57

"Dancing Mistress, The," 41–42
"Dead Mabelle," 44–45
Death of the Heart, The: Anna's role in, 14–15, 16, 19, 131, 132–33; art as theme in, 20, 23; authorship as theme in, 14–16, 132, 134–35; Brutt's role in, 13–14, 16, 17, 19, 20, 22, 23, 24, 113; Bursley's role in, 19, 22; Cecil's role in, 19; characterization in, 13–14, 18–19; Clara's role in, 19; Daphne's role in, 18–19, 20; Dickie's role in, 19; Eddie's role in, 13–14, 15–16, 17, 22, 23, 113; *Eva Trout* compared to, 120, 135, 138; female characters in, 132–34;

171

172   INDEX

Death of the Heart, The (continued)
Heat of the Day compared to, 131, 134;
Heccomb's role in, 18, 22; the home's importance in, 19–20, 21–22, 56; illusions
as theme in, 43; innocence vs. experience
as theme in, 13–14, 19, 20–21, 22, 23,
25, 39; Irene's role in, 18; language vs. silence as theme in, 126, 134; Lillian's role
in, 18, 22; Little Girls compared to, 113;
Matchett's role in, 17–18, 22, 23, 25; nature in, 20–21, 25; organization of, 13,
14, 20; Portia's role in, 13–14, 16–17, 20,
21, 22–23, 24–25, 131, 132, 133–34,
135; the Quaynes' roles in, 18, 19; St.
Quentin's role in, 14, 15, 16, 19, 21–22,
23, 120, 132, 134–35; setting of, 13;
Sound and the Fury compared to, 17; style
of, 13, 14, 19, 20, 23–24; Thomas's role
in, 14, 16–17; titles of sections, significance of, in, 22; tradition as theme in, 14,
17–18, 19, 20, 21, 23; war as theme in,
82; World of Love compared to, 105, 107,
108, 110
"Demon Lover, The," 108
Dickinson, Emily, 136
"Disinherited, The": Davina's role in, 47, 48;
general themes in, 47, 141–42, 143; the
home's importance in, 48; Marianne's role
in, 47–48, 108; Oliver's role in, 47, 48;
Prothero's role in, 47, 48; World of Love
compared to, 108
"Doll's House, The" (Mansfield), 145, 147–48
"Dry Salvages, The" (Eliot), 60

Earlham (Forster), 56
"East Coker" (Eliot), 56
"Easter Egg Party, The," 43
Eliot, George, 157
Eliot, T. S., 56, 60, 131
Elizabeth Bowen (Glendinning), 153, 155
Eva Trout: alienation as theme in, 104–5, 120,
121; authorship as theme in, 135, 137;
biblical allusions in, 136; the Bonnards'
roles in, 121; consolation sought in, 104;
Constantine's role in, 118, 119, 120, 121,
136; criticism of, 119, 120, 157; Death of
the Heart compared to, 120, 135, 137;
Elsinore's role in, 136; Eric's role in, 119;
Eva's role in, 118–20, 121–22, 124, 131,
135–38; film imagery in, 121–22; Heat of
the Day compared to, 131, 135, 137;
Henry's role in, 119, 120; "Her Table
Spread" compared to, 118; homosexuality
and lesbianism in, 120; innocence vs. experience as theme in, 120, 121; Iseult's role
in, 119, 120, 121, 124, 135, 136, 137;
Jeremy's role in, 119–20, 121–22, 137–
38; language vs. silence as theme in, 118,
119, 121, 122, 126, 135–38; "Last Night
in the Old Home" compared to, 118; Little Girls compared to, 115, 120; Louise's
role in, 119; names, significance of, in,
120, 136; style of, 119, 120–21; time and
memory as theme in, 105–6, 112, 121; To

the North compared to, 64, 119, 120; violence as theme in, 118, 119

Faulkner, William, 13
Flaubert, Gustave, 157, 158
"Foothold," 44
Forster, E. M., 87; and Bowen, 56, 84, 105,
120
Freud, Sigmund, 1, 142
Friends and Relations, 27, 35, 63, 105, 112
Frye, Northrop, 159

Glendinning, Victoria, 104, 153, 155
Green, Henry, 83, 105, 157
Greene, Graham, 105, 140, 157

Hamlet (Shakespeare), Heat of the Day compared to, 82, 84–85, 86, 87, 93, 94
"Happy Autumn Fields, The," 103, 106, 108,
112
Hartley, L. P., 105
Heath, William, 48, 58–59, 68, 91
Heat of the Day, The: Between the Acts compared to, 83; Brideshead Revisited compared to, 83; Caught compared to, 83;
class distinctions as theme in, 93, 95–96;
Connie's role in, 96; criticism of, 89–90;
Death of the Heart compared to, 131,
134; "Dry Salvages" compared to, 60; Eva
Trout compared to, 131, 135, 137; Hamlet compared to, 82, 84–85, 86, 87, 93,
94, 99; Harrison's role in, 83–84, 87, 91–
93, 97, 126, 129–30; the home's importance in, 57, 58–60, 87–89, 91–92, 93,
94–95, 96–97; innocence vs. experience as
theme in, 82, 85–86; Kelway's role in, 88;
King Lear compared to, 98, 99; language
vs. silence as theme in, 92, 97, 98–100,
125–27, 129–32, 134; Last September
compared to, 60; light and seeing as theme
in, 89, 97–98, 100; Louie's role in, 83,
95–96, 99, 100, 126–27, 128, 129–32;
madness as theme in, 94, 95, 96; Man and
Superman compared to, 87; names, significance of, in, 88, 125; Nettie's role in, 93,
94–95, 123–24, 126; religion in, 96; repression as theme in, 88; Robert's role in,
58, 59, 83, 84, 87, 88–91, 92, 95, 99,
100; Roderick's role in, 59, 60, 61, 84, 93,
99–100, 124; setting of, 83; Stella's role
in, 58, 83–84, 85–87, 90–91, 92, 93, 95,
96, 97, 99, 100, 125, 129–30, 131; style
of, 82–83, 84, 90, 92, 93; time and memory as theme in, 100; To the North compared to, 36; tradition as theme in, 93,
94–95, 100; treason and detection as
theme in, 89–90, 92–93, 96; war as theme
in, 82; Women in Love compared to, 90
"Her Table Spread," 118
Hidden from History (Rowbotham), 86
Homans, Margaret, 136, 137
Hotel, The, 55